NATIONAL LIBERATION, SOCIALISM AND IMPERIALISM

D0878131

NATIONAL LIBERATION, SOCIALISM AND IMPERIALISM

Selected Writings
by V. I. LENIN

INTERNATIONAL PUBLISHERS
New York

Copyright © *by* INTERNATIONAL PUBLISHERS CO., INC., 1968

Second Printing, 1970

SBN: (cloth) 7178-0110-1; (paperback) 7178-0135-7
Library of Congress Catalog Card Number: 68–9130
Printed in the United States of America

CONTENTS

THE NATIONAL PROGRAMME OF THE R.S.D.L.P.

The Conference of the Central Committee has adopted a resolution on the national question,* which has been printed in the "Notification",[1] and has placed the question of a national programme on the agenda of the Congress.

Why and how the national question has, at the present time, been brought to the fore—in the entire policy of the counter-revolution, in the class-consciousness of the bourgeoisie and in the proletarian Social-Democratic Party of Russia—is shown in detail in the resolution itself. There is hardly any need to dwell on this in view of the clarity of the situation. This situation and the fundamentals of a national programme for Social-Democracy have recently been dealt with in Marxist theoretical literature (the most prominent place being taken by Stalin's article[2]). We therefore consider that it will be to the point if, in this article, we confine ourselves to the presentation of the problem from a purely Party standpoint and to explanations that cannot be made in the legal press, crushed as it is by the Stolypin-Maklakov[3] oppression.

Social-Democracy in Russia is taking shape by drawing exclusively on the experience of older countries, i.e., of Europe, and on the theoretical expression of that experience, Marxism. The specific feature of our country and the specific features of the historical period of the establishment of Social-Democracy in our country are: first, in our country, as distinct from Europe, Social-Democracy began to take shape *before* the bourgeois revolution and continued taking shape *during* that revolution. Secondly, in our

---

* V. I. Lenin, *Collected Works*, Vol. 19, pp. 427-29.—*Ed.*

country the inevitable struggle to separate proletarian from general bourgeois and petty-bourgeois democracy—a struggle that is fundamentally the same as that experienced by every country—is being conducted under the conditions of a complete theoretical victory of Marxism in the West and in our country. The form taken by this struggle, therefore, is not so much that of a struggle for Marxism as a struggle for or against petty-bourgeois theories that are hidden behind "almost Marxist" phrases.

That is how the matter stands, beginning with Economism[4] (1895-1901) and "legal Marxism"[5] (1895-1901, 1902). Only those who shrink from historical truth can forget the close, intimate connection and relationship between these trends and Menshevism[6] (1903-07) and liquidationism[7] (1908-13).

In the national question the old *Iskra*,[8] which in 1901-03 worked on and completed a programme for the R.S.D.L.P. as well as laying the first and fundamental basis of Marxism in the theory and practice of the Russian working-class movement, had to struggle, in the same way as on other questions, against petty-bourgeois opportunism. This opportunism was expressed, first and foremost, in the nationalist tendencies and waverings of the Bund.[9] The old *Iskra* conducted a stubborn struggle against Bund nationalism, and to forget this is tantamount to becoming a Forgetful John again, and cutting oneself off from the historical and ideological roots of the whole Social-Democratic workers' movement in Russia.

On the other hand, when the Programme of the R.S.D.L.P. was finally adopted at the Second Congress in August 1903, there was a struggle, unrecorded in the Minutes of the Congress because it took place in the *Programme Commission*, which was visited by almost the entire Congress—a struggle against the clumsy attempts of several Polish Social-Democrats to cast doubts on "the right of nations to self-determination", i.e., attempts to deviate towards opportunism and nationalism from a quite different angle.

And today, ten years later, the struggle goes on along those same two basic *lines*, which shows equally that there is a profound connection between this struggle and all the objective conditions affecting the national question in Russia.

At the Brünn Congress in Austria (1899) the programme of "cultural-national autonomy" (defended by Kristan, Ellenbogen and others and expressed in the draft of the Southern Slavs) was *rejected*. *Territorial* national autonomy was adopted, and Social-Democratic propaganda for the obligatory union of all national regions was only a *compromise* with the idea of "cultural-national autonomy". The chief theoreticians of this unfortunate idea themselves lay particular emphasis on its *inapplicability* to Jewry.

In Russia—*as usual*—people have been found who have made it their business to enlarge on a little opportunist error and develop it into a system of opportunist policy. In the same way as Bernstein in Germany brought into being the Right Constitutional-Democrats in Russia—Struve, Bulgakov, Tugan & Co.—so Otto Bauer's "forgetfulness of internationalism" (as the supercautious Kautsky calls it!) *gave rise* in Russia to the *complete* acceptance of "cultural-national autonomy" *by all* the Jewish bourgeois parties and a large number of petty-bourgeois trends (the Bund and a *conference* of Socialist-Revolutionary national parties in 1907). Backward Russia serves, one might say, as an example of how the microbes of West-European opportunism produce whole *epidemics* on our savage soil.

In Russia people are fond of saying that Bernstein is "tolerated" in Europe, but they forget to add that nowhere in the world, with the exception of "holy" Mother Russia, has Bernsteinism engendered Struvism, or has "Bauerism" led to the justification, by Social-Democrats, of the refined nationalism of the Jewish bourgeoisie.

"Cultural-national autonomy" implies precisely the most refined and, therefore, the most harmful nationalism, it implies the corruption of the workers by means of the slogan of national culture and the propaganda of the profoundly harmful and even anti-democratic segregating of schools according to nationality. In short, this programme undoubtedly contradicts the internationalism of the proletariat and is in accordance only with the ideals of the nationalist petty bourgeoisie.

But there is *one case* in which the Marxists are duty bound, if they do not want to betray democracy and the

7

proletariat, to defend one special demand in the national question; that is, the *right* of nations to self-determination (§ 9 of the R.S.D.L.P. Programme), i.e., the right to political secession. The Conference resolution explains and motivates this demand in such detail that there is no place left for misunderstanding.

We shall, therefore, give only a brief description of those amazingly ignorant and opportunist objections that have been raised against this section of the Programme. In connection with this let us mention that *in the course of the ten years'* existence of the Programme *not one single unit* of the R.S.D.L.P., not one single national organisation, not one single regional conference, not one local committee and not one delegate to a congress or conference, has attempted to raise the question of changing or annulling § 9!

It is necessary to bear this in mind. It shows us at once whether there is a grain of seriousness or Party spirit in the objections raised to this point.

Take Mr. Semkovsky of the liquidators' newspaper. With the casual air of a man who has liquidated a party, he announces: "For certain reasons we do not share Rosa Luxemburg's proposal to remove § 9 from the Programme altogether" (*Novaya Rabochaya Gazeta* No. 71).

So the reasons are a secret! But then, how can secrecy be avoided in face of such ignorance of the history of our Programme? Or when that same Mr. Semkovsky, incomparably casual (what do the Party and the Programme matter!) makes an exception for Finland?

"What are we to do... if the Polish proletariat wants to carry on a joint struggle together with the whole proletariat of Russia within the framework of one state, and the reactionary classes of Polish society, on the contrary, want to separate Poland from Russia and, through a referendum, obtain a majority of votes in favour of separation; are we, Russian Social-Democrats, to vote in a central parliament together with our Polish comrades *against* secession, or, in order not to infringe on the 'right to self-determination', vote *in favour* of secession?"

What, indeed, are we to do when such naive and so hopelessly confused questions are raised?

The *right* to self-determination, my dear Mr. Liquidator, certainly does *not* imply the solution of the problem by a central parliament, but by a parliament, a diet, or a referendum of the *seceding minority*. When Norway seceded from Sweden (1905) it was decided by Norway *alone* (a country half the size of Sweden).

Even a child could see that Mr. Semkovsky is hopelessly mixed up.

"The right to self-determination" implies a democratic system *of a type* in which there is not only democracy in general, but specifically one in which there *could not be an undemocratic* solution of the question of secession. Democracy, speaking generally, is compatible with militant and tyrannical nationalism. The proletariat demands a democracy that *rules out* the forcible retention of any one of the nations within the bounds of the state. "In order not to infringe on the right to self-determination", therefore, we are duty bound *not* "to vote for secession", as the wily Mr. Semkovsky assumes, but to vote for the right of the seceding region to decide the question *itself*.

It would seem that even with Mr. Semkovsky's mental abilities it is not difficult to deduce that "the *right* to divorce" does not require that one should *vote* for divorce! But such is the fate of those who criticise § 9—they forget the ABC of logic.

At the time of Norway's secession from Sweden, the Swedish proletariat, if they did not want to follow the nationalist petty bourgeoisie, were *duty bound to vote* and agitate against the annexation of Norway by force, as the Swedish priesthood and landed proprietors desired. This is obvious and not too difficult to understand. Swedish nationalist democrats could refrain from a type of agitation that the principle of the *right* to self-determination demands of the proletariat of *ruling, oppressor nations*.

"What are we to do if the reactionaries are in the majority?" asks Mr. Semkovsky. This is a question worthy of a third form schoolboy. What is to be done about the *Russian* constitution if democratic voting gives the reactionaries a majority? Mr. Semkovsky asks idle, empty questions that have nothing to do with the matter in hand— they are the kind of questions that, as it is said, seven fools can ask more of than seventy wise men can answer.

When a democratic vote gives the reactionaries a majority, one of two things may, and usually does occur: either the decision of the reactionaries is implemented and its harmful consequences send the masses more or less speedily over to the side of democracy and against the reactionaries; or the conflict between democracy and reaction is decided by a civil or other war, which is also quite possible (and no doubt even the Semkovskys have heard of this) under a democracy.

The recognition of the right to self-determination is, Mr. Semkovsky assures us, "playing into the hands of the most thorough-paced bourgeois nationalism". This is childish nonsense since the recognition of the *right* does not exclude either propaganda and agitation *against* separation or the exposure of bourgeois nationalism. But it is absolutely indisputable that the denial of the *right* to secede is "playing into the hands" of the *most thorough-paced reactionary Great-Russian* nationalism!

This is the essence of Rosa Luxemburg's amusing error for which she was ridiculed a long time ago by German and Russian (August 1903) Social-Democrats; in their fear of playing into the hands of the bourgeois nationalism of oppressed nations, people play into the hands not merely of the bourgeois but of the reactionary nationalism of the *oppressor* nation.

If Mr. Semkovsky had not been so virginally innocent in matters concerning Party history and the Party Programme he would have understood that it was his duty to refute Plekhanov, who, *eleven years ago*, in defending the draft programme (which became the Programme in 1903) of the R.S.D.L.P. in *Zarya*,[10] made *a special point* (page 38) of the recognition of the right to self-determination and wrote the following about it:

"This demand, which is not obligatory for bourgeois democrats, even in theory, is obligatory for us as Social-Democrats. If we were to forget about it or were afraid to put it forward for fear of impinging on the national prejudices of our compatriots of Great-Russian origin, the battle-cry of world Social-Democracy, 'Workers of all countries, unite!' would be a shameful lie upon our lips."

As long ago as the *Zarya* days, Plekhanov put forward the basic argument which was developed in detail in the conference resolution, an argument to which the Semkovskys have not attempted to draw attention for eleven years. In Russia there are 43 per cent Great Russians, but Great-Russian nationalism rules over the other 57 per cent of the population and oppresses all nations. The National-Liberals (Struve & Co., the Progressists, etc.) have already joined forces with our national-reactionaries and the "first swallows" of *national* democracy have appeared (remember Mr. Peshekhonov's appeal in August 1906 to be cautious in our attitude to the nationalist prejudices of the muzhik).

In Russia only the liquidators consider the bourgeois-democratic revolution to be over, and the concomitant of *such* a revolution all over the world always has been and still is national movements. In Russia in particular there are oppressed nations in many of the border regions, which in neighbouring states enjoy greater liberty. Tsarism is more reactionary than the neighbouring states, constitutes the *greatest* barrier to free economic development, and does its utmost to foster Great-Russian nationalism. For a Marxist, of course, *all other conditions being equal*, big states are always preferable to small ones. But it would be ridiculous and reactionary even to suppose that conditions under the tsarist monarchy might be equal to those in any European country or any but a minority of Asian countries.

The denial of the right of nations to self-determination in present-day Russia is, therefore, undoubted opportunism and a refusal to fight against the reactionary Great-Russian nationalism that is still all-powerful.

Sotsial-Demokrat No. 32,
December 15 (28), 1913

Collected Works, Vol. 19

CRITICAL REMARKS
ON THE NATIONAL QUESTION[11]

It is obvious that the national question has now become prominent among the problems of Russian public life. The aggressive nationalism of the reactionaries, the transition of counter-revolutionary bourgeois liberalism to nationalism (particularly Great-Russian, but also Polish, Jewish, Ukrainian, etc.), and lastly, the increase of nationalist vacillations among the different "national" (i.e., non-Great-Russian) Social-Democrats, who have gone to the length of violating the Party Programme—all these make it incumbent on us to give more attention to the national question than we have done so far.

This article pursues a special object, namely, to examine, in their general bearing, precisely these programme vacillations of Marxists and would-be Marxists, on the national question. In *Severnaya Pravda*[12] No. 29 (for September 5, 1913, "Liberals and Democrats on the Language Question"*) I had occasion to speak of the opportunism of the liberals on the national question; this article of mine was attacked by the opportunist Jewish newspaper *Zeit*,[13] in an article by Mr. F. Liebman. From the other side, the programme of the Russian Marxists on the national question has been criticised by the Ukrainian opportunist Mr. Lev Yurkevich (*Dzvin*,[14] 1913, Nos. 7-8). Both these writers touched upon so many questions that to reply to them we are obliged to deal with the most diverse aspects of the subject. I think the most convenient thing would be to start with a reprint of the article from *Severnaya Pravda*.

---

* See V. I. Lenin, *Collected Works*, Vol. 19, pp. 354-57.—*Ed.*

1. Liberals and Democrats on the Language Question

On several occasions the newspapers have mentioned the report of the Governor of the Caucasus, a report that is noteworthy, not for its Black-Hundred[15] spirit, but for its timid "liberalism". Among other things, the Governor objects to artificial Russification of non-Russian nationalities. Representatives of non-Russian nationalities in the Caucasus are *themselves* striving to teach their children Russian; an example of this is the Armenian church schools, in which the teaching of Russian is not obligatory.

Russkoye Slovo[16] (No. 198), one of the most widely circulating liberal newspapers in Russia, points to this fact and draws the correct conclusion that the hostility towards the Russian language in Russia "stems exclusively from" the "artificial" (it should have said "forced") implanting of that language.

"There is no reason to worry about the fate of the Russian language. It will itself win recognition throughout Russia," says the newspaper. This is perfectly true, because the requirements of economic exchange will always compel the nationalities living in one state (as long as they wish to live together) to study the language of the majority. The more democratic the political system in Russia becomes, the more powerfully, rapidly and extensively capitalism will develop, the more urgently will the requirements of economic exchange impel various nationalities to study the language most convenient for general commercial relations.

The liberal newspaper, however, hastens to slap itself in the face and demonstrate its liberal inconsistency.

"Even those who oppose Russification," it says, "would hardly be likely to deny that in a country as huge as Russia there must be one single official language, and that this language can be only Russian."

Logic turned inside out! Tiny Switzerland has not lost anything, but has gained from having not *one single* official language, but three—German, French and Italian. In Switzerland 70 per cent of the population are Germans (in Russia 43 per cent are Great Russians), 22 per cent French (in Russia 17 per cent are Ukrainians) and 7 per cent Italians (in Russia 6 per cent are Poles and 4.5 per cent Byelorussians). If Italians in Switzerland often speak

13

French in their common parliament they do not do so because they are menaced by some savage police law (there are none such in Switzerland), but because the civilised citizens of a democratic state themselves prefer a language that is understood by a majority. The French language does not instil hatred in Italians because it is the language of a free civilised nation, a language that is not imposed by disgusting police measures.

Why should "huge" Russia, a much more varied and terribly backward country, *inhibit* her development by the retention of any kind of privilege for any one language? Should not the contrary be true, liberal gentlemen? Should not Russia, if she wants to overtake Europe, put an end to every kind of privilege as quickly as possible, as completely as possible and as vigorously as possible?

If all privileges disappear, if the imposition of any one language ceases, all Slavs will easily and rapidly learn to understand each other and will not be frightened by the "horrible" thought that speeches in different languages will be heard in the common parliament. The requirements of economic exchange will themselves *decide* which language of the given country it is to the *advantage* of the majority to know in the interests of commercial relations. This decision will be all the firmer because it is adopted voluntarily by a population of various nationalities, and its adoption will be the more rapid and extensive the more consistent the democracy and, as a consequence of it, the more rapid the development of capitalism.

The liberals approach the language question in the same way as they approach all political questions—like hypocritical hucksters, holding out one hand (openly) to democracy and the other (behind their backs) to the feudalists and police. We are against privileges, shout the liberals, and under cover they haggle with the feudalists for first one, then another, privilege.

Such is the nature of *all* liberal-bourgeois nationalism—not only Great-Russian (it is the worst of them all because of its violent character and its kinship with the Purishkeviches), but Polish, Jewish, Ukrainian, Georgian and every other nationalism. Under the slogan of "national culture" the bourgeoisie of *all* nations, both in Austria and in Russia, are *in fact* pursuing the policy of splitting the workers, emasculating democracy and haggling with the feudalists over the sale of the people's rights and the people's liberty.

The slogan of working-class democracy is not "national culture" but the international culture of democracy and the world-wide working-class movement. Let the bourgeoisie deceive the people with various "positive" national programmes. The class-conscious worker will answer the bourgeoisie—there is only one solution to the national problem (insofar as it can, in general, be solved in the capitalist world, the world of profit, squabbling and exploitation), and that solution is consistent democracy.

The proof—Switzerland in Western Europe, a country with an old culture, and Finland in Eastern Europe, a country with a young culture.

The national programme of working-class democracy is: absolutely no privileges for any one nation or any one language; the solution of the problem of the political self-determination of nations, that is, their separation as states by completely free, democratic methods; the promulgation of a law for the whole state by virtue of which any measure (rural, urban or communal, etc., etc.) introducing any privilege of any kind for one of the nations and militating against the equality of nations or the rights of a national minority, shall be declared illegal and ineffective, and any citizen of the state shall have the right to demand that such a measure be annulled as unconstitutional, and that those who attempt to put it into effect be punished.

Working-class democracy contraposes to the nationalist wrangling of the various bourgeois parties over questions of language, etc., the demand for the unconditional unity and complete amalgamation of workers of *all* nationalities in *all* working-class organisations—trade union, co-operative, consumers', educational and all others—in contradistinction to any kind of bourgeois nationalism. Only this type of unity and amalgamation can uphold democracy and defend the interests of the workers against capital—which is already international and is becoming more so—and promote the development of mankind towards a new way of life that is alien to all privileges and all exploitation.

2. "National Culture"

As the reader will see, the article in *Severnaya Pravda* made use of a particular example, i.e., the problem of the official language, to illustrate the inconsistency and opportunism of the liberal bourgeoisie, which, in the national question, extends a hand to the feudalists and the police. Everybody will understand that, apart from the problem of an official language, the liberal bourgeoisie behaves just as treacherously, hypocritically and stupidly (even from the standpoint of the interests of liberalism) in a number of other related issues.

The conclusion to be drawn from this? It is that *all* liberal-bourgeois nationalism sows the greatest corruption among the workers and does immense harm to the cause of freedom and the proletarian class struggle. This bourgeois (and bourgeois-feudalist) tendency is all the more dangerous for its *being concealed* behind the slogan of "national culture". It is under the guise of national culture —Great-Russian, Polish, Jewish, Ukrainian, and so forth—that the Black-Hundreds and the clericals, and also the bourgeoisie of *all* nations, are doing their dirty and reactionary work.

Such are the facts of the national life of today, if viewed from the Marxist angle, i.e., from the standpoint of the class struggle, and if the slogans are compared with the interests and policies of classes, and not with meaningless "general principles", declamations and phrases.

The slogan of national culture is a bourgeois (and often also a Black-Hundred and clerical) fraud. Our slogan is: the international culture of democracy and of the world working-class movement.

Here the Bundist Mr. Liebman rushes into the fray and annihilates me with the following deadly tirade:

"Anyone in the least familiar with the national question knows that international culture is not non-national culture (culture without a national form); non-national culture, which must not be Russian, Jewish, or Polish, but only pure culture, is nonsense; international ideas can appeal to the working class only when they are adapted to the language spoken by the worker, and to the concrete national conditions under which he lives; the worker should not be indifferent to the condition and development of his national culture, because it is through it, and only through it, that he is able to participate in the 'international culture of democracy and of the world working-class movement'. This is well known, but V. I. turns a deaf ear to it all...."

Ponder over this typically Bundist argument, designed, if you please, to demolish the Marxist thesis that I advanced. With the air of supreme self-confidence of one who is "familiar with the national question", this Bundist passes off ordinary bourgeois views as "well-known" axioms.

It is true, my dear Bundist, that international culture is not non-national. Nobody said that it was. Nobody has proclaimed a "pure" culture, either Polish, Jewish, or Russian, etc., and your jumble of empty words is simply an attempt to distract the reader's attention and to obscure the issue with tinkling words.

The *elements* of democratic and socialist culture are present, if only in rudimentary form, in *every* national culture, since in *every* nation there are toiling and exploited masses, whose conditions of life inevitably give rise to the ideology of democracy and socialism. But *every* nation also possesses a bourgeois culture (and most nations a reactionary and clerical culture as well) in the form, not merely of "elements", but of the *dominant* culture. Therefore, the general "national culture" *is* the culture of the landlords, the clergy and the bourgeoisie. This fundamental and, for a Marxist, elementary truth, was kept in the background by the Bundist, who "drowned" it in his jumble of words, i.e., *instead of* revealing and clarifying the class gulf to the reader, he in fact obscured it. *In fact*, the Bundist acted like a bourgeois, whose every interest requires the spreading of a belief in a non-class national culture.

In advancing the slogan of "the international culture of democracy and of the world working-class movement", we take *from each* national culture *only* its democratic and socialist elements; we take them *only* and *absolutely* in opposition to the bourgeois culture and the bourgeois nationalism of *each* nation. No democrat, and certainly no Marxist, denies that all languages should have equal status, or that it is necessary to polemise with one's "native" bourgeoisie in one's native language and to advocate anti-clerical or anti-bourgeois ideas among one's

17

"native" peasantry and petty bourgeoisie. That goes without saying, but the Bundist uses these indisputable truths to obscure the point in dispute, i.e., the real issue.

The question is whether it is permissible for a Marxist, directly or indirectly, to advance the slogan of national culture, or whether he should *oppose* it by advocating, in all languages, the slogan of workers' *internationalism* while "adapting" himself to all local and national features.

The significance of the "national culture" slogan is not determined by some petty intellectual's promise, or good intention, to "interpret" it as "meaning the development through it of an international culture". It would be puerile subjectivism to look at it in that way. The significance of the slogan of national culture is determined by the objective alignment of all classes in a given country, and in all countries of the world. The national culture of the bourgeoisie is a *fact* (and, I repeat, the bourgeoisie everywhere enters into deals with the landed proprietors and the clergy). Aggressive bourgeois nationalism, which drugs the minds of the workers, stultifies and disunites them in order that the bourgeoisie may lead them by the halter—such is the fundamental fact of the times.

Those who seek to serve the proletariat must unite the workers of all nations, and unswervingly fight bourgeois nationalism, *domestic* and foreign. The place of those who advocate the slogan of national culture is among the nationalist petty bourgeois, not among the Marxists.

Take a concrete example. Can a Great-Russian Marxist accept the slogan of national, Great-Russian, culture? No, he cannot. Anyone who does that should stand in the ranks of the nationalists, not of the Marxists. Our task is to fight the dominant, Black-Hundred and bourgeois national culture of the Great Russians, and to develop, exclusively in the internationalist spirit and in the closest alliance with the workers of other countries, the rudiments also existing in the history of our democratic and working-class movement. Fight your own Great-Russian landlords and bourgeoisie, fight their "culture" in the name of internationalism, and, in so fighting, "adapt" yourself to the special features of the Purishkeviches and Struves—that is your task, not preaching or tolerating the slogan of national culture.

The same applies to the most oppressed and persecuted nation—the Jews. Jewish national culture is the slogan of the rabbis and the bourgeoisie, the slogan of our enemies. But there are other elements in Jewish culture and in Jewish history as a whole. Of the ten and a half million Jews in the world, somewhat over a half live in Galicia and Russia, backward and semi-barbarous countries, where the Jews are *forcibly* kept in the status of a caste. The other half lives in the civilised world, and there the Jews do not live as a segregated caste. There the great world-progressive features of Jewish culture stand clearly revealed: its internationalism, its identification with the advanced movements of the epoch (the percentage of Jews in the democratic and proletarian movements is everywhere higher than the percentage of Jews among the population).

Whoever, directly or indirectly, puts forward the slogan of Jewish "national culture" is (whatever his good intentions may be) an enemy of the proletariat, a supporter of all that is *outmoded* and connected with *caste* among the Jewish people; he is an accomplice of the rabbis and the bourgeoisie. On the other hand, those Jewish Marxists who mingle with the Russian, Lithuanian, Ukrainian and other workers in international Marxist organisations, and make their contribution (both in Russian and in Yiddish) towards creating the international culture of the working-class movement—those Jews, despite the separatism of the Bund, uphold the best traditions of Jewry by fighting the slogan of "national culture".

Bourgeois nationalism and proletarian internationalism— these are the two irreconcilably hostile slogans that correspond to the two great class camps throughout the capitalist world, and express the *two* policies (nay, the two world outlooks) in the national question. In advocating the slogan of national culture and building up on it an entire plan and practical programme of what they call "cultural-national autonomy", the Bundists are *in effect* instruments of bourgeois nationalism among the workers.

3. The Nationalist Bogey of "Assimilation"

The question of assimilation, i.e., of the shedding of national features, and absorption by another nation, strikingly illustrates the consequences of the nationalist vacillations of the Bundists and their fellow-thinkers.

Mr. Liebman, who faithfully conveys and repeats the stock arguments, or rather, tricks, of the Bundists, has qualified as "the *old assimilation story*" the demand for the unity and amalgamation of the workers of all nationalities in a given country in united workers' organisations (see the concluding part of the article in *Severnaya Pravda*).

"Consequently," says Mr. F. Liebman, commenting on the concluding part of the article in *Severnaya Pravda*, "if asked what nationality he belongs to, the worker must answer: I am a Social-Democrat."

Our Bundist considers this the acme of wit. As a matter of fact, he gives himself away completely by *such* witticisms and outcries about "assimilation", *levelled against* a consistently democratic and *Marxist* slogan.

Developing capitalism knows two historical tendencies in the national question. The first is the awakening of national life and national movements, the struggle against all national oppression, and the creation of national states. The second is the development and growing frequency of international intercourse in every form, the break-down of national barriers, the creation of the international unity of capital, of economic life in general, of politics, science, etc.

Both tendencies are a universal law of capitalism. The former predominates in the beginning of its development, the latter characterises a mature capitalism that is moving towards its transformation into socialist society. The Marxists' national programme takes both tendencies into account, and advocates, firstly, the equality of nations and languages and the impermissibility of all *privileges* in this respect (and also the right of nations to self-determination, with which we shall deal separately later); secondly, the principle of internationalism and uncompromising struggle against contamination of the proletariat with bourgeois nationalism, even of the most refined kind.

The question arises: what does our Bundist mean when

he cries out to heaven against "assimilation"? He *could not* have meant the oppression of nations, or the *privileges* enjoyed by a particular nation, because the word "assimilation" here does not fit at all, because all Marxists, individually, and as an official, united whole, have quite definitely and unambiguously condemned the slightest violence against and oppression and inequality of nations, and finally because this general Marxist idea, which the Bundist has attacked, is expressed in the *Severnaya Pravda* article in the most emphatic manner.

No, evasion is impossible here. In condemning "assimilation" Mr. Liebman had in mind, *not* violence, *not* inequality, and *not* privileges. Is there anything real left in the concept of assimilation, after all violence and all inequality have been eliminated?

Yes, there undoubtedly is. What is left is capitalism's world-historical tendency to break down national barriers, obliterate national distinctions, and to *assimilate* nations— a tendency which manifests itself more and more powerfully with every passing decade, and is one of the greatest driving forces transforming capitalism into socialism.

Whoever does not recognise and champion the equality of nations and languages, and does not fight against all national oppression or inequality, is not a Marxist; he is not even a democrat. That is beyond doubt. But it is also beyond doubt that the pseudo-Marxist who heaps abuse upon a Marxist of another nation for being an "assimilator" is simply a *nationalist philistine*. In this unhandsome category of people are all the Bundists and (as we shall shortly see) Ukrainian nationalist-socialists such as L. Yurkevich, Dontsov and Co.

To show concretely how reactionary the views held by these nationalist philistines are, we shall cite facts of three kinds.

It is the Jewish nationalists in Russia in general, and the Bundists in particular, who vociferate most about Russian orthodox Marxists being "assimilators". And yet, as the afore-mentioned figures show, out of the ten and a half million Jews all over the world, *about half* that number live in the *civilised* world, where conditions favouring "assimilation" are *strongest*, whereas the unhappy, downtrodden, disfranchised Jews in Russia and Galicia, who are crushed under the heel of the Purishkeviches (Russian and Polish), live where conditions for "assimilation" *least* prevail, where there is most segregation, and even a "Pale of Settlement",[17] a *numerus clausus*[18] and other charming features of the Purishkevich regime.

The Jews in the civilised world are not a nation, they have in the main become assimilated, say Karl Kautsky and Otto Bauer. The Jews in Galicia and in Russia are not a nation; unfortunately (through *no* fault of their own but through that of the Purishkeviches), they are still a *caste* here. Such is the incontrovertible judgement of people who are undoubtedly familiar with the history of Jewry and take the above-cited facts into consideration.

What do these facts prove? It is that only Jewish reactionary philistines, who want to turn back the wheel of history, and make it proceed, not from the conditions prevailing in Russia and Galicia to those prevailing in Paris and New York, but in the reverse direction—only they can clamour against "assimilation".

The best Jews, those who are celebrated in world history, and have given the world foremost leaders of democracy and socialism, have never clamoured against assimilation. It is only those who contemplate the "rear aspect" of Jewry with reverential awe that clamour against assimilation.

A rough idea of the scale which the general process of assimilation of nations is assuming under the present conditions of advanced capitalism may be obtained, for example, from the immigration statistics of the United States of America. During the decade between 1891-1900, Europe sent 3,700,000 people there, and during the nine years between 1901 and 1909, 7,200,000. The 1900 census in the United States recorded over 10,000,000 foreigners. New York State, in which, according to the same census, there were over 78,000 Austrians, 136,000 Englishmen, 20,000 Frenchmen, 480,000 Germans, 37,000 Hungarians, 425,000 Irish, 182,000 Italians, 70,000 Poles, 166,000 people from Russia (mostly Jews), 43,000 Swedes, etc., grinds down national distinctions. And what is taking place on a grand, international scale in New York is also to be seen in *every* big city and industrial township.

No one unobsessed by nationalist prejudices can fail to

perceive that this process of assimilation of nations by capitalism means the greatest historical progress, the breakdown of hidebound national conservatism in the various backwoods, especially in backward countries like Russia.

Take Russia and the attitude of Great Russians towards the Ukrainians. Naturally, every democrat, not to mention Marxists, will strongly oppose the incredible humiliation of Ukrainians, and demand complete equality for them. But it would be a downright betrayal of socialism and a silly policy *even* from the standpoint of the bourgeois "national aims" of the Ukrainians to *weaken* the ties and the alliance between the Ukrainian and Great-Russian proletariat that now exist within the confines of a single state.

Mr. Lev Yurkevich, who calls himself a "Marxist" (poor Marx!), is an example of that silly policy. In 1906, Sokolovsky (Basok) and Lukashevich (Tuchapsky) asserted, Mr. Yurkevich writes, that the Ukrainian proletariat had become completely Russified and needed no separate organisation. Without quoting a single fact *bearing on the direct issue*, Mr. Yurkevich falls upon both for saying this and cries out hysterically—quite in the spirit of the basest, most stupid and most reactionary nationalism—that this is "national passivity", "national renunciation", that these men have "split [!!] the Ukrainian Marxists", and so forth. Today, despite the "growth of Ukrainian national consciousness among the workers", the *minority* of the workers are "nationally conscious", while the majority, Mr. Yurkevich assures us, "are still under the influence of Russian culture". And it is our duty, this nationalist philistine exclaims, "not to follow the masses, but to lead them, to explain to them their national aims (*natsionalna sprava*)" (*Dzvin,* p. 89).

This argument of Mr. Yurkevich's is wholly bourgeois-nationalistic. But even from the point of view of the bourgeois nationalists, some of whom stand for complete equality and autonomy for the Ukraine, while others stand for an independent Ukrainian state, this argument will not wash. The Ukrainians' striving for liberation is opposed by the Great-Russian and Polish landlord class and by the bourgeoisie of these two nations. What social force is capable of standing up to these classes? The first decade of the twentieth century provided an actual reply to this question: that force is none other than the working class, which rallies the democratic peasantry behind it. By striving to divide, and thereby weaken, the genuinely democratic force, whose victory would make national oppression impossible, Mr. Yurkevich is betraying, not only the interests of democracy in general, but also the interests of his own country, the Ukraine. Given united action by the Great-Russian and Ukrainian proletarians, a free Ukraine *is possible;* without such unity, it is out of the question.

But Marxists do not confine themselves to the bourgeois-national standpoint. For several decades a well-defined process of accelerated economic development has been going on in the South, i.e., the Ukraine, attracting hundreds of thousands of peasants and workers from Great Russia to the capitalist farms, mines, and cities. The "assimilation"—within these limits—of the Great-Russian and Ukrainian proletariat is an indisputable fact. *And this* fact is *undoubtedly* progressive. Capitalism is replacing the ignorant, conservative, settled muzhik of the Great-Russian or Ukrainian backwoods with a mobile proletarian whose conditions of life break down specifically national narrow-mindedness, both Great-Russian and Ukrainian. Even if we assume that, in time, there will be a state frontier between Great Russia and the Ukraine, the historically progressive nature of the "assimilation" of the Great-Russian and Ukrainian workers will be as undoubted as the progressive nature of the grinding down of nations in America. The freer the Ukraine and Great Russia become, the *more extensive and more rapid* will be the development of capitalism, which will still more powerfully attract the workers, the working masses of *all* nations from all regions of the state and from all the neighbouring states (should Russia become a neighbouring state in relation to the Ukraine) to the cities, the mines, and the factories.

Mr. Lev Yurkevich acts like a real bourgeois, and a short-sighted, narrow-minded, obtuse bourgeois at that, i.e., like a philistine, when he dismisses the benefits to be gained from the intercourse, amalgamation and assimilation of the *proletariat* of the two nations, for the sake of the momentary success of the Ukrainian national cause (*sprava*). The national cause comes first and the proletarian cause second, the bourgeois nationalists say, with the Yurkeviches, Dontsovs and similar would-be Marxists repeating it after them. The proletarian cause must come first, we say, because it not only protects the lasting and fundamental interests of labour and of humanity, but also those of democracy; and without democracy neither an autonomous nor an independent Ukraine is conceivable.

Another point to be noted in Mr. Yurkevich's argument, which is so extraordinarily rich in nationalist gems, is this: the minority of Ukrainian workers are nationally conscious, he says; "the majority are still under the influence of Russian culture" (*bilshist perebuvaye shche pid vplyvom rosiiskoi kultury*).

Contraposing Ukrainian culture as a whole to Great-Russian culture as a whole, when speaking of the proletariat, is a gross betrayal of the proletariat's interests for the benefit of bourgeois nationalism.

There are two nations in every modern nation—we say to all nationalist-socialists. There are two national cultures in every national culture. There is the Great-Russian culture of the Purishkeviches, Guchkovs and Struves—but there is also the Great-Russian culture typified in the names of Chernyshevsky and Plekhanov. There are *the same two* cultures in the Ukraine as there are in Germany, in France, in England, among the Jews, and so forth. If the majority of the Ukrainian workers are under the influence of Great-Russian culture, we also know definitely that the ideas of Great-Russian democracy and Social-Democracy operate parallel with the Great-Russian clerical and bourgeois culture. In fighting the latter kind of "culture", the Ukrainian *Marxist* will always bring the former into focus, and say to his workers: "We must snatch at, make use of, and develop to the utmost every opportunity for intercourse with the Great-Russian class-conscious workers, with their literature and with their range of ideas; the fundamental interests of *both* the Ukrainian and the Great-Russian working-class movements demand it."

If a Ukrainian Marxist allows himself to be swayed by his *quite legitimate and natural* hatred of the Great-Russian oppressors *to such a degree* that he transfers even a particle of this hatred, even if it be only estrangement, to the proletarian culture and proletarian cause of the Great-Russian workers, then such a Marxist will get bogged down in bourgeois nationalism. Similarly, the Great-Russian Marxists will be bogged down, not only in bourgeois, but also in Black-Hundred nationalism, if he loses sight, even for a moment, of the demand for complete equality for the Ukrainians, or of their *right* to form an independent state.

The Great-Russian and Ukrainian workers must work together, and, as long as they live in a single state, act in the closest organisational unity and concert, towards a common or international culture of the proletarian movement, displaying absolute tolerance in the question of the language in which propaganda is conducted, and in the purely local or purely national *details* of that propaganda. This is the imperative demand of Marxism. All advocacy of the segregation of the workers of one nation from those of another, all attacks upon Marxist "assimilation", or attempts, where the proletariat is concerned, to contrapose one national culture as a whole to another allegedly integral national culture, and so forth, is *bourgeois* nationalism, against which it is essential to wage a ruthless struggle.

4. "Cultural-National Autonomy"

The question of the "national culture" slogan is of enormous importance to Marxists, not only because it determines the ideological content of all our propaganda and agitation on the national question, as distinct from bourgeois propaganda, but also because the entire programme of the much-discussed cultural-national autonomy is based on this slogan.

The main and fundamental flaw in this programme is that it aims at introducing the most refined, most absolute and most extreme nationalism. The gist of this programme is that every citizen registers as belonging to a particular nation, and every nation constitutes a legal entity with the right to impose compulsory taxation on its members, with national parliaments (Diets) and national secretaries of state (ministers).

Such an idea, applied to the national question, resembles Proudhon's idea, as applied to capitalism. Not abolishing capitalism and its basis—commodity production—but *purg-ing* that basis of abuses, of excrescences, and so forth; not abolishing exchange and exchange value, but, on the con-trary, making it "constitutional", universal, absolute, *"fair"*, and free of fluctuations, crises and abuses—such was Proud-hon's idea.

Just as Proudhon was petty-bourgeois, and his theory converted exchange and commodity production into an absolute category and exalted them as the acme of perfec-tion, so is the theory and programme of "cultural-national autonomy" petty-bourgeois, for it converts bourgeois na-tionalism into an absolute category, exalts it as the acme of perfection, and purges it of violence, injustice, etc.

Marxism cannot be reconciled with nationalism, be it even of the "most just", "purest", most refined and civilised brand. In place of all forms of nationalism Marxism ad-vances internationalism, the amalgamation of all nations in the higher unity, a unity that is growing before our eyes with every mile of railway line that is built, with every international trust, and every workers' association that is formed (an association that is international in its economic activities as well as in its ideas and aims).

The principle of nationality is historically inevitable in bourgeois society and, taking this society into due account, the Marxist fully recognises the historical legitimacy of na-tional movements. But to prevent this recognition from becoming an apologia of nationalism, it must be strictly limited to what is progressive in such movements, in order that this recognition may not lead to bourgeois ideology obscuring proletarian consciousness.

The awakening of the masses from feudal lethargy, and their struggle against all national oppression, for the sovereignty of the people, of the nation, are progressive. Hence, it is the Marxist's *bounden* duty to stand for the most resolute and consistent democratism on all aspects of the national question. This task is largely a negative one. But this is the limit the proletariat can go to in supporting nationalism, for beyond that begins the "positive" activity of the *bourgeoisie* striving to *fortify* nationalism.

To throw off the feudal yoke, all national oppression, and all privileges enjoyed by any particular nation or lan-guage, is the imperative duty of the proletariat as a democratic force, and is certainly in the interests of the proletarian class struggle, which is obscured and retarded by bickering on the national question. But to go *beyond* these strictly limited and definite historical limits in helping bourgeois nationalism means betraying the proletariat and siding with the bourgeoisie. There is a border-line here, which is often very slight and which the Bundists and Ukrainian nationalist-socialists completely lose sight of.

Combat all national oppression? Yes, of course! Fight *for* any kind of national development, *for* "national culture" in general?—Of course not. The economic development of capitalist society presents us with examples of immature national movements all over the world, examples of the formation of big nations out of a number of small ones, or to the detriment of some of the small ones, and also examples of the assimilation of nations. The development of nationality in general is the principle of bourgeois nationalism; hence the exclusiveness of bourgeois nationalism, hence the endless national bickering. The proletariat, however, far from undertaking to uphold the national development of every nation, on the contrary, warns the masses against such illusions, stands for the fullest freedom of capitalist intercourse and welcomes every kind of assimilation of nations, except that which is founded on force or privilege.

Consolidating nationalism within a certain "justly" delimited sphere, "constitutionalising" nationalism, and securing the separation of all nations from one another by means of a special state institution—such is the ideological foundation and content of cultural-national autonomy. This idea is thoroughly bourgeois and thoroughly false. The proletariat cannot support any consecration of nationalism; on the contrary, it supports everything that helps to obliterate national distinctions and remove national barriers: it supports everything that makes the ties between nationalities closer and closer, or tends to merge nations. To act differently means siding with reactionary nationalist philistinism.

When, at their Congress in Brünn (in 1899), the Austrian Social-Democrats discussed the plan for cultural-national autonomy, practically no attention was paid to a theoretical appraisal of that plan. It is, however, noteworthy that the following two arguments were levelled against this programme: (1) it would tend to strengthen clericalism; (2) "its result would be the perpetuation of chauvinism, its introduction into every small community, into every small group" (p. 92 of the official report of the Brünn Congress, in German. A Russian translation was published by the Jewish nationalist party, the J.S.L.P.[19]).

There can be no doubt that "national culture", in the ordinary sense of the term, i.e., schools, etc., is at present under the predominant influence of the clergy and the bourgeois chauvinists in all countries in the world. When the Bundists, in advocating "cultural-national" autonomy, say that the constituting of nations will keep the class struggle within them *clean* of all extraneous considerations, then that is manifest and ridiculous sophistry. It is primarily in the economic and political sphere that a serious class struggle is waged in any capitalist society. To separate the sphere of education *from this* is, firstly, absurdly utopian, because schools (like "national culture" in general) cannot be separated from economics and politics; secondly, it is the economic and political life of a capitalist country that *necessitates* at every step the smashing of the absurd and outmoded national barriers and prejudices, whereas separation of the school system and the like, would only perpetuate, intensify and strengthen "pure" clericalism and "pure" bourgeois chauvinism.

On the boards of joint-stock companies we find capitalists of different nations sitting together in complete harmony. At the factories workers of different nations work side by side. In any really serious and profound political issue sides are taken according to classes, not nations. "Withdrawing" school education and the like "from state control" and placing it under the control of the nations is in effect an attempt to *separate* from economics, which unites the nations, the most highly, so to speak, ideological sphere of social life, the sphere in which "pure" national culture or the national cultivation of clericalism and chauvinism has the freest play.

In practice, the plan for "extra-territorial" or "cultural-national" autonomy could mean only one thing: *the division of educational affairs according to nationality,* i.e., the introduction of national curias in school affairs. Sufficient thought to the *real* significance of the famous Bund plan will enable one to realise how utterly reactionary it is even from the standpoint of democracy, let alone from that of the proletarian class struggle for socialism.

A single instance and a single scheme for the "nationalisation" of the school system will make this point abundantly clear. In the United States of America the division of the States into Northern and Southern holds to this day in all departments of life; the former possess the greatest traditions of freedom and of struggle against the slaveowners; the latter possess the greatest traditions of slaveownership, survivals of persecution of the Negroes, who are economically oppressed and culturally backward (44 per cent of Negroes are illiterate, and 6 per cent of whites), and so forth. In the Northern States Negro children attend the same schools as white children do. In the South there are separate "national", or racial, whichever you please, schools for Negro children. I think that this is the sole instance of actual "nationalisation" of schools.

In Eastern Europe there exists a country where things like the Beilis case[20] are still possible, and Jews are condemned by the Purishkeviches to a condition worse than that of the Negroes. In that country a scheme for *nationalising Jewish schools* was recently mooted in the Ministry. Happily, this reactionary utopia is no more likely to be realised than the utopia of the Austrian petty bourgeoisie, who have despaired of achieving consistent democracy or of putting an end to national bickering, and have invented for the nations school-education *compartments* to keep them from bickering *over the distribution* of schools... but have "constituted" themselves for an *eternal* bickering of one "national culture" with another.

In Austria, the idea of cultural-national autonomy has remained largely a flight of literary fancy, which the Austrian Social-Democrats themselves have not taken seriously. In Russia, however, it has been incorporated in the programmes of all the Jewish bourgeois parties, and of several petty-bourgeois, opportunist elements in the different nations—for example, the Bundists, the liquidators in the Caucasus, and the conference of Russian national parties of the Left-Narodnik trend. (This conference, we will mention parenthetically, took place in 1907, its decision being adopted *with abstention* on the part of the Russian Socialist-Revolutionaries[21] and the P.S.P.,[22] the Polish social-patriots. Abstention from voting is a method surprisingly characteristic of the Socialist-Revolutionaries and P.S.P., when they want to show their attitude towards a most important question of principle in the sphere of the national programme!)

In Austria it was Otto Bauer, the principal theoretician of "cultural-national autonomy", who devoted a special chapter of his book to prove that such a programme cannot possibly be proposed for the Jews. In Russia, however, it is precisely among the Jews that all the bourgeois parties—and the Bund which echoes them—have adopted this programme.* What does this go to show? It goes to show that history, through the political practice of another state, has exposed the absurdity of Bauer's invention, in exactly the same way as the Russian Bernsteinians (Struve, Tugan-Baranovsky, Berdyaev and Co.), through their rapid evolution from Marxism to liberalism, have exposed the real ideological content of the German Bernsteinism.[25]

Neither the Austrian nor the Russian Social-Democrats have incorporated "cultural-national" autonomy in their programme. However, the Jewish bourgeois parties in a most backward country, and a number of petty-bourgeois, so-called socialist groups *have adopted it* in order to spread ideas of bourgeois nationalism among the working class in a refined form. This fact speaks for itself.

----

* That the Bundists often vehemently deny that *all* the Jewish bourgeois parties have accepted "cultural-national autonomy" is understandable. This fact only too glaringly exposes the actual role being played by the Bund. When Mr. Manin, a Bundist, tried, in *Luch*,[23] to repeat his denial, he was fully exposed by N. Skop (see *Prosveshcheniye* No. 3[24]). But when Mr. Lev Yurkevich, in *Dzvin* (1913, No. 7-8, p. 92), quotes from *Prosveshcheniye* (No. 3, p. 78) N. Sk.'s statement that "the Bundists together with all the Jewish bourgeois parties and groups have long been advocating cultural-national autonomy" and *distorts* this statement by *dropping* the word "Bundists", and *substituting* the words "national rights" for the words "cultural-national autonomy", one can only raise one's hands in amazement! Mr. Lev Yurkevich is not only a nationalist, not only an astonishing ignoramus in matters concerning the history of the Social-Democrats and their programme, but a *downright falsifier of quotations* for the benefit of the Bund. The affairs of the Bund and the Yurkeviches must be in a bad way indeed!

Since we have had to touch upon the Austrian programme on the national question, we must reassert a truth which is often distorted by the Bundists. At the Brünn Congress a *pure* programme of "cultural-national autonomy" *was* presented. This was the programme of the South-Slav Social-Democrats, §2 of which reads: "Every nation living in Austria, irrespective of the territory occupied by its members, constitutes an autonomous group which manages all its national (language and cultural) affairs quite independently." This programme was supported, not only by Kristan but by the influential Ellenbogen. But it was withdrawn; not a single vote was cast for it. A *territorialist* programme was adopted, i.e., one that did *not* create *any* national groups "irrespective of the territory occupied by the members of the nation".

Clause 3 of the adopted programme reads: "The self-governing *regions* of one and the same nation shall jointly form a nationally united association, which shall manage its national affairs on an absolutely autonomous basis" (cf. *Prosveshcheniye,* 1913, No. 4, p. 28). Clearly, this compromise programme is wrong too. An example will illustrate this. The German colonists' community in Saratov Gubernia, plus the German working-class suburb of Riga or Lodz, plus the German housing estate near St. Petersburg, etc., would constitute a "nationally united association" of Germans in Russia. Obviously the Social-Democrats cannot *demand* such a thing or *enforce* such an association, although of course they do not in the least deny *freedom* of every kind of association, including associations of any communities of any nationality in a given state. The segregation, by a law of the state, of Germans, etc., in different localities and of different classes in Russia into a single German-national association may be practised by anybody —priests, bourgeois or philistines, but not by Social-Democrats.

5. The Equality of Nations and the Rights of National Minorities

When they discuss the national question, opportunists in Russia are given to citing the example of Austria. In my article in *Severnaya* Pravda* (No. 10 *Prosveshcheniye*, pp. 96-98), which the opportunists have attacked (Mr. Semkovsky in *Novaya Rabochaya Gazeta*,[26] and Mr. Liebman in *Zeit*), I asserted that, insofar as that is at all possible under capitalism, there was only one solution of the national question, viz., through consistent democracy. In proof of this, I referred, among other things, to Switzerland.

This has not been to the liking of the two opportunists mentioned above, who are trying to refute it or belittle its significance. Kautsky, we are told, said that Switzerland is an exception; Switzerland, if you please, has a special kind of decentralisation, a special history, special geographical conditions, unique distribution of a population that speak different languages, etc., etc.

All these are nothing more than attempts to *evade* the issue. To be sure, Switzerland is an exception in that she is not a single-nation state. But Austria and Russia are also exceptions (or are backward, as Kautsky adds). To be sure, it was only her special, unique historical and social conditions that ensured Switzerland *greater* democracy than most of her European neighbours.

But where does all this come in, if we are speaking of the *model* to be adopted? In the whole world, under present-day conditions, countries in which any particular institution has been founded on *consistent* democratic principles are the exception. Does this prevent us, in our programme, from upholding consistent democracy in all institutions?

Switzerland's special features lie in her history, her geographical and other conditions. Russia's special features lie in the strength of her proletariat, which has no precedent in the epoch of bourgeois revolutions, and in her shocking general backwardness, which objectively necessitates an exceptionally rapid and resolute advance, under the threat of all sorts of drawbacks and reverses.

We are evolving a national programme from the proletarian standpoint; since when has it been recommended that the worst examples, rather than the best, be taken as a model?

At all events, does it not remain an indisputable and undisputed fact that national peace under capitalism has been

---

* See this pamphlet, pp. 13-15.—*Ed.*

achieved (insofar as it is achievable) *exclusively* in countries where consistent democracy prevails?

Since this is indisputable, the opportunists' persistent references to Austria instead of Switzerland are nothing but a typical Cadet device, for the Cadets always copy the worst European constitutions rather than the best.

In Switzerland there are *three* official languages, but bills submitted to a referendum are printed in *five* languages, that is to say, in two Romansh dialects, in addition to the three official languages. According to the 1900 census, these two dialects are spoken by 38,651 out of the 3,315,443 inhabitants of Switzerland, i.e., by a little over *one per cent*. In the army, commissioned and non-commissioned officers "are given the fullest freedom to speak to the men in their native language". In the cantons of Graubünden and Wallis (each with a population of a little over a hundred thousand) both dialects enjoy complete equality.*

The question is: should we advocate and support this, the living *experience* of an advanced country, or borrow from the Austrians *inventions* like "extra-territorial autonomy", which have not yet been tried out anywhere in the world (and not yet been adopted by the Austrians themselves)?

To advocate this invention is to advocate the division of school education according to nationality, and that is a downright harmful idea. The experience of Switzerland proves, however, that the greatest (relative) degree of national peace *can be, and has been, ensured in practice* where you have a consistent (again relative) democracy throughout the state.

"In Switzerland," say people who have studied this question, "there is *no national question* in the East-European sense of the term. The very phrase (national question) is unknown there...." "Switzerland left the struggle between nationalities a long way behind, in 1797-1803."**

This means that the epoch of the great French Revolution, which provided the most democratic solution of the

---

* See René Henry: *La Suisse et la question des langues*, Berne, 1907.
** See Ed. Blocher: *Die Nationalitäten in der Schweiz*, Berlin, 1910.

current problems of the transition from feudalism to capitalism, *succeeded* incidentally, en passant, in *"solving"* the national question.

Let the Semkovskys, Liebmans, and other opportunists now try to assert that this "exclusively Swiss" solution is *inapplicable* to any uyezd or even part of an uyezd in Russia, where out of a population of only 200,000 forty thousand speak *two dialects* and want to have *complete equality* of language in their area!

Advocacy of complete equality of nations and languages distinguishes only the consistently democratic elements in each nation (i.e., only the proletarians), and *unites* them, not according to nationality, but in a profound and earnest desire to improve the entire system of state. On the contrary, advocacy of "cultural-national autonomy", despite the pious wishes of individuals and groups, *divides the nations* and in fact draws the workers and the bourgeoisie of any one nation closer together (the adoption of this "cultural-national autonomy" by all the Jewish bourgeois parties).

Guaranteeing the rights of a national minority is inseparably linked up with the principle of complete equality. In my article in *Severnaya Pravda* this principle was expressed in almost the same terms as in the later, official and more accurate decision of the conference of Marxists. That decision demands "the incorporation in the constitution of a fundamental law which shall declare null and void all privileges enjoyed by any one nation and all infringements of the rights of a national minority."

Mr. Liebman tries to ridicule this formula and asks: "Who knows what the rights of a national minority are?" Do these rights, he wants to know, include the right of the minority to have "its own programme" for the national schools? How large must the national minority be to have the right to have its own judges, officials, and schools with instruction in its own language? Mr. Liebman wants it to be inferred from these questions that a *"positive"* national programme is essential.

Actually, these questions clearly show what reactionary ideas our Bundist tries to smuggle through under cover of a dispute on supposedly minor details and particulars.

"Its own programme" in its national schools!... Marxists, my dear nationalist-socialist, have a *general* school programme which demands, for example, an absolutely secular school. As far as Marxists are concerned, no *departure* from this general programme is anywhere or at any time permissible in a democratic state (the question of introducing any "local" subjects, languages, and so forth into it being decided by the local inhabitants). However, from the principle of "taking educational affairs out of the hands of the state" and placing them under the control of the nations, it ensues that we, the workers, must allow the "nations" in our democratic state to spend the people's money on clerical schools! Without being aware of the fact, Mr. Liebman has clearly demonstrated the reactionary nature of "cultural-national autonomy"!

"How large must a national minority be?" This is not defined even in the Austrian programme, of which the Bundists are enamoured. It says (more briefly and less clearly than our programme does): "The rights of the national minorities are protected by a special law to be passed by the Imperial Parliament" (§4 of the Brünn programme).

Why has nobody asked the Austrian Social-Democrats the question: what exactly is that law, and exactly which rights and of which minority is it to protect?

That is because all sensible people understand that it is inappropriate and impossible to define particulars in a programme. A programme lays down only fundamental principles. In this case the fundamental principle is implied with the Austrians, and directly expressed in the decision of the latest conference of Russian Marxists. That principle is: no national privileges and no national inequality.

Let us take a concrete example to make the point clear to the Bundist. According to the school census of January 18, 1911, St. Petersburg elementary schools under the Ministry of Public "Education" were attended by 48,076 pupils. Of these, 396, i.e., less than one per cent, were Jews. The other figures are: Rumanian pupils—2, Georgians—1, Armenians—3, etc.[27] It is possible to draw up a "positive" national programme that will cover this diversity of relationships and conditions? (And St. Petersburg is, of course, far from being the city with the most mixed population in

Russia.) Even such specialists in national "subtleties" as the Bundists would hardly be able to draw up such a programme.

And yet, if the constitution of the country contained a fundamental law rendering null and void every measure that infringed the rights of a minority, any citizen would be able to demand the rescinding of orders prohibiting, for example, the hiring, at state expense, of special teachers of Hebrew, Jewish history, and the like, or the provision of state-owned premises for lectures for Jewish, Armenian, or Rumanian children, or even for the one Georgian child. At all events, it is by no means impossible to meet, on the basis of equality, all the reasonable and just wishes of the national minorities, and nobody will say that advocacy of equality is harmful. On the other hand, it would certainly be harmful to advocate division of schools according to nationality, to advocate, for example, special schools for Jewish children in St. Petersburg, and it would be utterly impossible to set up national schools for *every* national minority, for one, two or three children.

Furthermore, it is impossible, in any country-wide law, to define how large a national minority must be to be entitled to special schools, or to special teachers for supplementary subjects, etc.

On the other hand, a country-wide law establishing equality can be worked out in detail and developed through special regulations and the decisions of regional Diets, and town, Zemstvo, village commune and other authorities.

6. Centralisation and Autonomy

In his rejoinder, Mr. Liebman writes:

"Take our Lithuania, the Baltic province, Poland, Volhynia, South Russia, etc.—everywhere you will find a *mixed* population; there is not a single city that does not have a large national minority. However far decentralisation is carried out, different nationalities will always be found living together in different places (chiefly in urban communities), and it is democratism that surrenders a national minority to the national majority. But, as we know, V. I. is opposed to the federal state structure and the boundless decentralisation that exist in the Swiss Federation. The question is: what was his point in citing the example of Switzerland?"

My object in citing the example of Switzerland has already been explained above. I have also explained that the problem of protecting the rights of a national minority can be solved *only* by a country-wide law promulgated in a consistently democratic state that does not depart from the principle of equality. But in the passage quoted above, Mr. Liebman repeats still another of the most common (and most fallacious) arguments (or sceptical remarks) which are usually made against the Marxist national programme, and which, therefore, deserve examination.

Marxists are, of course, opposed to federation and decentralisation, for the simple reason that capitalism requires for its development the largest and most centralised possible states. *Other conditions being equal*, the class-conscious proletariat will always stand for the larger state. It will always fight against medieval particularism, and will always welcome the closest possible economic amalgamation of large territories in which the proletariat's struggle against the bourgeoisie can develop on a broad basis.

Capitalism's broad and rapid development of the productive forces *calls for* large, politically compact and united territories, since only here can the bourgeois class—together with its inevitable antipode, the proletarian class—unite and sweep away all the old, medieval, caste, parochial, petty-national, religious and other barriers.

The right of nations to self-determination, i.e., the right to secede and form independent national states, will be dealt with elsewhere.* But while, and insofar as, different nations constitute a single state, Marxists will never, under any circumstances, advocate either the federal principle or decentralisation. The great centralised state is a tremendous historical step forward from medieval disunity to the future socialist unity of the whole world, and only *via* such a state (*inseparably* connected with capitalism), can there be any road to socialism.

It would, however, be inexcusable to forget that in advocating centralism we advocate exclusively *democratic* centralism. On this point all the philistines in general, and the nationalist philistines in particular (including the late Dra-

---

* See this pamphlet, pp. 45-104.—*Ed.*

gomanov[28]), have so confused the issue that we are obliged again and again to spend time clarifying it.

Far from precluding local self-government, with *autonomy* for regions having special economic and social conditions, a distinct national composition of the population, and so forth, democratic centralism necessarily demands *both*. In Russia centralism is constantly confused with tyranny and bureaucracy. This confusion has naturally arisen from the history of Russia, but even so it is quite inexcusable for a Marxist to yield to it.

This can best be explained by a concrete example.

In her lengthy article "The National Question and Autonomy",* Rosa Luxemburg, among many other curious errors (which we shall deal with below), commits the exceptionally curious one of trying to *restrict* the demand for autonomy to Poland alone.

But first let us see *how* she defines autonomy.

Rosa Luxemburg admits—and being a Marxist she is of course bound to admit—that all the major and important economic and political questions of capitalist society must be dealt with exclusively by the central parliament of the whole country concerned, not by the autonomous Diets of the individual regions. These questions include tariff policy, laws governing commerce and industry, transport and means of communication (railways, post, telegraph, telephone, etc.), the army, the taxation system, civil** and criminal law, the general principles of education (for example, the law on purely secular schools, on universal education, on the minimum programme, on democratic school management, etc.), the labour protection laws, and political liberties (right of association), etc., etc.

The autonomous Diets—on the basis of the general laws of the country—should deal with questions of purely local, regional, or national significance. Amplifying this idea in great—not to say excessive—detail, Rosa Luxemburg mentions, for example, the construction of local railways (No. 12, p. 149) and local highways (No. 14-15, p. 376), etc.

---

* *Przeglad Socjaldemokratyczny,*[29] Kraków, 1908 and 1909.
** In elaborating her ideas Rosa Luxemburg goes into details, mentioning, for example—and quite rightly—divorce laws (No. 12, p. 162 of the above-mentioned journal).

Obviously, one cannot conceive of a modern, truly democratic state that did *not* grant such autonomy to every region having any appreciably distinct economic and social features, populations of a specific national composition, etc. The principle of centralism, which is essential for the development of capitalism, is not violated by this (local and regional) autonomy, but on the contrary is applied by it *democratically*, not bureaucratically. The broad, free and rapid development of capitalism would be impossible, or at least greatly impeded, by the *absence* of such autonomy, which *facilitates* the concentration of capital, the development of the productive forces, the unity of the bourgeoisie and the unity of the proletariat on a *country-wide* scale; for bureaucratic interference in *purely* local (regional, national, and other) questions is one of the greatest obstacles to economic and political development in general, and an obstacle to *centralism* in serious, important and fundamental matters in particular.

One cannot help smiling, therefore, when reading how our magnificent Rosa Luxemburg tries to prove, with a very serious air and "purely Marxist" phrases, that the demand for autonomy is applicable *only* to Poland and *only* by way of exception! Of course, there is not a grain of "parochial" patriotism in this; we have here only "practical" considerations ... in the case of Lithuania, for example.

Rosa Luxemburg takes four gubernias—Vilna, Kovno, Grodno and Suvalki—assuring her readers (and herself) that these are inhabited "mainly" by Lithuanians; and by adding the inhabitants of these gubernias together she finds that Lithuanians constitute 23 per cent of the total population, and if Zhmuds are added, they constitute 31 per cent—less than a third. The natural inference is that the idea of autonomy for Lithuania is "arbitrary and artificial" (No. 10, p. 807).

The reader who is familiar with the commonly known defects of our Russian official statistics will quickly see Rosa Luxemburg's mistake. Why take Grodno Gubernia where the Lithuanians constitute only 0.2 per cent, *one-fifth of one per cent*, of the population? Why take the whole Vilna Gubernia and not its Troki Uyezd alone, where the Lithuanians constitute the *majority* of the population?

Why take the whole Suvalki Gubernia and put the number of Lithuanians at 52 per cent of the population, and not the Lithuanian uyezds of that gubernia, i.e., five out of the seven, in which Lithuanians constitute 72 per cent of the population?

It is ridiculous to talk about the conditions and demands of modern capitalism while at the same time taking not the "modern", not the "capitalist", but the medieval, feudal and official-bureaucratic administrative divisions of Russia, and in their crudest form at that (gubernias instead of uyezds). Plainly, there can be no question of any serious local reform in Russia until these divisions are abolished and superseded by a *really* "modern" division that really meets the requirements, *not* of the Treasury, *not* of the bureaucracy, *not* of routine, *not* of the landlords, *not* of the priests, but of capitalism; and one of the modern requirements of capitalism is undoubtedly the greatest possible national uniformity of the population, for nationality and language identity are an important factor making for the complete conquest of the home market and for complete freedom of economic intercourse.

Oddly enough, this obvious mistake of Rosa Luxemburg's is repeated by the Bundist Medem, who sets out to prove. not that Poland's specific features are "exceptional", but that the principle of national-territorial autonomy is unsuitable (the Bundists stand for national extra-territorial autonomy!). Our Bundists and liquidators collect from all over the world all the errors and all the opportunist vacillations of Social-Democrats of different countries and different nations and appropriate to themselves the *worst* they can find in world Social-Democracy. A scrap-book of Bundist and liquidator writings could, taken together, serve as a model Social-Democratic *museum of bad taste*.

Regional autonomy, Medem tells us didactically, is good for a region or a "territory", but not for Lettish, Estonian, or other areas (*okrugs*), which have populations ranging from half a million to two million and areas equal to a gubernia. *"That would not be autonomy, but simply a Zemstvo....* Over this Zemstvo it would be necessary to establish real autonomy"... and the author goes on to condemn the "break-up" of the old gubernias and uyezds.*

As a matter of fact, the preservation of the medieval, feudal, official administrative divisions means the "break-up" and mutilation of the conditions of modern capitalism. Only people imbued with the spirit of these divisions can, with the learned air of the expert, speculate on the contraposition of "Zemstvo" and "autonomy", calling for the stereotyped application of "autonomy" to large regions and of the Zemstvo to small ones. Modern capitalism does not demand these bureaucratic stereotypes at all. Why national areas with populations, not only of half a million, but even of 50,000, should not be able to enjoy autonomy; why such areas should not be able to unite in the most diverse ways with neighbouring areas of different dimensions into a single autonomous "territory" if that is convenient or necessary for economic intercourse—these things remain the secret of the Bundist Medem.

We would mention that the Brünn Social-Democratic national programme is based entirely on national-territorial autonomy; it proposes that Austria should be divided into "nationally distinct" areas "instead of the historical crown lands" (Clause 2 of the Brünn programme). We would not go as far as that. A uniform national population is undoubtedly one of the most reliable factors making for free, broad and really modern commercial intercourse. It is beyond doubt that not a single Marxist, and not even a single firm democrat, will stand up for the Austrian crown lands and the Russian gubernias and uyezds (the latter are not as bad as the Austrian crown lands, but they are very bad nevertheless), or challenge the necessity of replacing these obsolete divisions by others that will conform as far as possible with the national composition of the population. Lastly, it is beyond doubt that in order to eliminate all national oppression it is very important to create autonomous areas, however small, with entirely homogeneous populations, towards which members of the respective nationalities scattered all over the country, or even all over the world, could gravitate, and with which

---

* V. Medem, "A Contribution to the Presentation of the National Question in Russia", *Vestnik Yevropy*,[30] 1912, Nos. 8 and 9.

they could enter into relations and free associations of every kind. All this is indisputable, and can be argued against only from the hidebound, bureaucratic point of view.

The national composition of the population, however, is *one* of the very important economic factors, *but not the sole and not* the most important factor. Towns, for example, play an *extremely important* economic role under capitalism, and everywhere, in Poland, in Lithuania, in the Ukraine, in Great Russia, and elsewhere, the towns are marked by mixed populations. To cut the towns off from the villages and areas that economically gravitate towards them, for the sake of the "national" factor, would be absurd and impossible. That is why Marxists must not take their stand entirely and exclusively on the "national-territorial" principle.

The solution of the problem proposed by the last conference of Russian Marxists is far more correct than the Austrian. On this question, the conference advanced the following proposition:

"this ... calls for wide regional autonomy [not for Poland alone, of course, but for all the regions of Russia]* and fully democratic local self-government, with the boundaries of the self-governing and autonomous regions determined [not by the boundaries of the present gubernias, uyezds, etc., but] by the local inhabitants themselves on the basis of their economic and social conditions, national make-up of the population, etc."**

Here the national composition of the population is placed on *the same level* as the other conditions (economic first, then social, etc.) which must serve as a basis for determining the new boundaries that will meet the needs of modern capitalism, not of bureaucracy and Asiatic barbarism. The local population alone can "assess" those conditions with full precision, and on that basis the central parliament of the country will determine the boundaries of the autonomous regions and the powers of autonomous Diets.

* * *

---

* Interpolations in square brackets (within passages quoted by Lenin) are by Lenin, unless otherwise indicated.—*Ed.*
** See V. I. Lenin, *Collected Works*, Vol. 19, pp. 427-28.—*Ed.*

We have still to examine the question of the right of nations to self-determination. On this question a whole collection of opportunists of all nationalities—the liquidator Semkovsky, the Bundist Liebman and the Ukrainian nationalist-socialist Lev Yurkevich—have set to work to "popularise" the errors of Rosa Luxemburg. This question, which has been so utterly confused by this whole "collection", will be dealt with in our next article.

Written in October-December 1913

Published in 1913, in the journal *Prosveshcheniye* Nos. 10, 11 and 12
Signed: *V. Ilyin*

Collected Works, Vol. 20

THE RIGHT OF NATIONS
TO SELF-DETERMINATION

Clause 9 of the Russian Marxists' Programme, which deals with the right of nations to self-determination, has (as we have already pointed out in *Prosveshcheniye*)* given rise lately to a crusade on the part of the opportunists. The Russian liquidator Semkovsky, in the St. Petersburg liquidationist newspaper, and the Bundist Liebman and the Ukrainian nationalist-socialist Yurkevich in their respective periodicals have violently attacked this clause and treated it with supreme contempt. There is no doubt that this campaign of a motley array of opportunists against our Marxist Programme is closely connected with present-day nationalist vacillations in general. Hence we consider a detailed examination of this question timely. We would mention, in passing, that none of the opportunists named above has offered a single argument of his own; they all merely repeat what Rosa Luxemburg said in her lengthy Polish article of 1908-09, "The National Question and Autonomy". In our exposition we shall deal mainly with the "original" arguments of this last-named author.

1. What Is Meant by the Self-Determination of Nations?

Naturally, this is the first question that arises when any attempt is made at a Marxist examination of what is known as self-determination. What should be understood by that

---

* See this pamphlet, pp. 12-44.—*Ed.*

term? Should the answer be sought in legal definitions deduced from all sorts of "general concepts" of law? Or is it rather to be sought in a historico-economic study of the national movements?

It is not surprising that the Semkovskys, Liebmans and Yurkeviches did not even think of raising this question, and shrugged it off by scoffing at the "obscurity" of the Marxist Programme, apparently unaware, in their simplicity, that the self-determination of nations is dealt with, not only in the Russian Programme of 1903,[31] but in the resolution of the London International Congress of 1896 (with which I shall deal in detail in the proper place). Far more surprising is the fact that Rosa Luxemburg, who declaims a great deal about the supposedly abstract and metaphysical nature of the clause in question, should herself succumb to the sin of abstraction and metaphysics. It is Rosa Luxemburg herself who is continually lapsing into generalities about self-determination (to the extent even of philosophising amusingly on the question of how the will of the nation is to be ascertained), without anywhere clearly and precisely asking herself whether the gist of the matter lies in legal definitions or in the experience of the national movements throughout the world.

A precise formulation of this question, which no Marxist can avoid, would at once destroy nine-tenths of Rosa Luxemburg's arguments. This is not the first time that national movements have arisen in Russia, nor are they peculiar to that country alone. Throughout the world, the period of the final victory of capitalism over feudalism has been linked up with national movements. For the complete victory of commodity production, the bourgeoisie must capture the home market, and there must be politically united territories whose population speak a single language, with all obstacles to the development of that language and to its consolidation in literature eliminated. Therein is the economic foundation of national movements. Language is the most important means of human intercourse. Unity and unimpeded development of language are the most important conditions for genuinely free and extensive commerce on a scale commensurate with modern capitalism, for a free and broad grouping of the population in all its various classes and, lastly, for the establishment of a close connection between the market and each and every proprietor, big or little, and between seller and buyer.

Therefore, the tendency of every national movement is towards the formation of *national states*, under which these requirements of modern capitalism are best satisfied. The most profound economic factors drive towards this goal, and, therefore, for the whole of Western Europe, nay, for the entire civilised world, the national state is *typical* and normal for the capitalist period.

Consequently, if we want to grasp the meaning of self-determination of nations, not by juggling with legal definitions, or "inventing" abstract definitions, but by examining the historico-economic conditions of the national movements, we must inevitably reach the conclusion that the self-determination of nations means the political separation of these nations from alien national bodies, and the formation of an independent national state.

Later on we shall see still other reasons why it would be wrong to interpret the right to self-determination as meaning anything but the right to existence as a separate state. At present, we must deal with Rosa Luxemburg's efforts to "dismiss" the inescapable conclusion that profound economic factors underlie the urge towards a national state.

Rosa Luxemburg is quite familiar with Kautsky's pamphlet *Nationality and Internationality*. (Supplement to *Die Neue Zeit*[32] No. 1, 1907-08; Russian translation in the journal *Nauchnaya Mysl*, Riga, 1908.) She is aware that, after carefully analysing the question of the national state in § 4 of that pamphlet, Kautsky arrived at the conclusion that Otto Bauer "*underestimates* the strength of the urge towards a national state" (p. 23 of the pamphlet). Rosa Luxemburg herself quotes the following words of Kautsky's: "The national state is the form *most suited* to present-day conditions, [i.e., capitalist, civilised, economically progressive conditions, as distinguished from medieval, pre-capitalist, etc.]; it is the form in which the state can best fulfil its tasks" (i.e., the tasks of securing the freest, widest and speediest development of capitalism). To this we must add Kautsky's still more precise concluding remark that states of mixed national composition (known as multinational states, as distinct from national states) are "always those whose internal constitution has for some reason or other remained abnormal or underdeveloped" (backward). Needless to say, Kautsky speaks of abnormality exclusively in the sense of lack of conformity with what is best adapted to the requirements of a developing capitalism.

The question now is: How did Rosa Luxemburg treat these historico-economic conclusions of Kautsky's? Are they right or wrong? Is Kautsky right in his historico-economic theory, or is Bauer, whose theory is basically psychological? What is the connection between Bauer's undoubted "national opportunism", his defence of cultural-national autonomy, his nationalistic infatuation ("an occasional emphasis on the national aspect", as Kautsky put it), his "enormous exaggeration of the national aspect and complete neglect of the international aspect" (Kautsky)— and his underestimation of the strength of the urge to create a national state?

Rosa Luxemburg has not even raised this question. She has not noticed the connection. She has not considered the *sum total* of Bauer's theoretical views. She has not even drawn a line between the historico-economic and the psychological theories of the national question. She confines herself to the following remarks in criticism of Kautsky:

"This 'best' national state is only an abstraction, which can easily be developed and defended theoretically, but which does not correspond to reality. (*Przeglad Socjaldemokratyczny*, 1908, No. 6, p. 499.)

And in corroboration of this emphatic statement there follow arguments to the effect that the "right to self-determination" of small nations is made illusory by the development of the great capitalist powers and by imperialism. "Can one seriously speak," Rosa Luxemburg exclaims, "about the 'self-determination' of the formally independent Montenegrins, Bulgarians, Rumanians, Serbs, Greeks, partly even the Swiss, whose independence is itself a result of the political struggle and the diplomatic game of the 'concert of Europe'?!" (P. 500.) The state that best suits these conditions is "not a national state, as Kautsky believes, but a predatory one". Some dozens of figures are quoted relating to the size of British, French and other colonial possessions.

After reading such arguments, one cannot help marvelling at the author's ability to misunderstand *the how and the why of things*. To teach Kautsky, with a serious mien, that small states are economically dependent on big ones, that a struggle is raging among the bourgeois states for the predatory suppression of other nations, and that imperialism and colonies exist—all this is a ridiculous and puerile attempt to be clever, for none of this has the slightest bearing on the subject. Not only small states, but even Russia, for example, is entirely dependent, economically, on the power of the imperialist finance capital of the "rich" bourgeois countries. Not only the miniature Balkan states, but even nineteenth-century America was, economically, a colony of Europe, as Marx pointed out in *Capital*.[33] Kautsky, like any Marxist, is, of course, well aware of this, but that has nothing whatever to do with the question of national movements and the national state.

For the question of the political self-determination of nations and their independence as states in bourgeois society, Rosa Luxemburg has substituted the question of their economic independence. This is just as intelligent as if someone, in discussing the programmatic demand for the supremacy of parliament, i.e., the assembly of people's representatives, in a bourgeois state, were to expound the perfectly correct conviction that big capital dominates in a bourgeois country, whatever the regime in it.

There is no doubt that the greater part of Asia, the most densely populated continent, consists either of colonies of the "Great Powers", or of states that are extremely dependent and oppressed as nations. But does this commonly-known circumstance in any way shake the undoubted fact that in Asia itself the conditions for the most complete development of commodity production and the freest, widest and speediest growth of capitalism have been created only in Japan, i.e., only in an independent national state? The latter is a bourgeois state, and for that reason has itself begun to oppress other nations and to enslave colonies. We cannot say whether Asia will have had time to develop into a system of independent national states, like Europe,

before the collapse of capitalism, but it remains an undisputed fact that capitalism, having awakened Asia, has
called forth national movements everywhere in that continent, too; that the tendency of these movements is towards
the creation of national states in Asia; that it is such states
that ensure the best conditions for the development of
capitalism. The example of Asia speaks *in favour* of Kautsky
and *against* Rosa Luxemburg.

The example of the Balkan states likewise contradicts
her, for anyone can now see that the best conditions for the
development of capitalism in the Balkans are created precisely in proportion to the creation of independent national
states in that peninsula.

Therefore, Rosa Luxemburg notwithstanding, the example
of the whole of progressive and civilised mankind, the
example of the Balkans and that of Asia prove that
Kautsky's proposition is absolutely correct: the national
state is the rule and the "norm" of capitalism; the multinational state represents backwardness, or is an exception.
From the standpoint of national relations, the best conditions for the development of capitalism are undoubtedly
provided by the national state. This does not mean, of
course, that such a state, which is based on bourgeois relations, can eliminate the exploitation and oppression of
nations. It only means that Marxists cannot lose sight of
the powerful *economic* factors that give rise to the urge to
create national states. It means that "self-determination of
nations" in the Marxists' Programme *cannot*, from a
historico-economic point of view, have any other meaning
than political self-determination, state independence, and
the formation of a national state.

The conditions under which the bourgeois-democratic
demand for a "national state" should be supported from a
Marxist, i.e., class-proletarian, point of view will be dealt
with in detail below. For the present, we shall confine
ourselves to the definition of the *concept* of "self-determination", and only note that Rosa Luxemburg *knows* what this
concept means ("national state"), whereas her opportunist
partisans, the Liebmans, the Semkovskys, the Yurkeviches,
do not even know that!

2. The Historically Concrete Presentation of the Question

The categorical requirement of Marxist theory in investigating any social question is that it be examined within *definite* historical limits, and, if it refers to a particular country (e.g., the national programme for a given country), that account be taken of the specific features distinguishing that country from others in the same historical epoch.

What does this categorical requirement of Marxism imply in its application to the question under discussion?

First of all, it implies that a clear distinction must be drawn between the two periods of capitalism, which differ radically from each other as far as the national movement is concerned. On the one hand, there is the period of the collapse of feudalism and absolutism, the period of the formation of the bourgeois-democratic society and state, when the national movements for the first time become mass movements and in one way or another draw *all* classes of the population into politics through the press, participation in representative institutions, etc. On the other hand, there is the period of fully formed capitalist states with a long-established constitutional regime and a highly developed antagonism between the proletariat and the bourgeoisie—a period that may be called the eve of capitalism's downfall.

The typical features of the first period are: the awakening of national movements and the drawing of the peasants, the most numerous and the most sluggish section of the population, into these movements, in connection with the struggle for political liberty in general, and for the rights of the nation in particular. Typical features of the second period are: the absence of mass bourgeois-democratic movements and the fact that developed capitalism, in bringing closer together nations that have already been fully drawn into commercial intercourse, and causing them to intermingle to an increasing degree, brings the antagonism between internationally united capital and the international working-class movement into the forefront.

Of course, the two periods are not walled off from each other; they are connected by numerous transitional links, the various countries differing from each other in the rapidity of their national development, in the national make-up and distribution of their population, and so on. There can be no question of the Marxists of any country drawing up their national programme without taking into account all these general historical and concrete state conditions.

It is here that we come up against the weakest point in Rosa Luxemburg's arguments. With extraordinary zeal, she embellishes her article with a collection of hard words directed against § 9 of our Programme, which she declares to be "sweeping", "a platitude", "a metaphysical phrase", and so on without end. It would be natural to expect an author who so admirably condemns metaphysics (in the Marxist sense, i.e., anti-dialectics) and empty abstractions to set us an example of how to make a concrete historical analysis of the question. The question at issue is the national programme of the Marxists of a definite country—Russia, in a definite period—the beginning of the twentieth century. But does Rosa Luxemburg raise the question as to *what historical* period Russia is passing through, or *what are the concrete* features of the national question and the national movements of that *particular* country in that *particular* period?

No, she does not! *She says absolutely nothing about it*! In her work you will not find even the shadow of an analysis of how the national question stands in *Russia* in the present historical period, or of the specific features of *Russia* in this particular respect!

We are told that the national question in the Balkans is presented differently from that in Ireland; that Marx appraised the Polish and Czech national movements in the concrete conditions of 1848 in such and such a way (a page of excerpts from Marx); that Engels appraised the struggle of the forest cantons of Switzerland against Austria and the Battle of Morgarten which took place in 1315 in such and such a way (a page of quotations from Engels with the appropriate comments from Kautsky); that Lassalle regarded the peasant war in Germany of the sixteenth century as reactionary, etc.

It cannot be said that these remarks and quotations have any novelty about them, but at all events it is interesting for the reader to be occasionally reminded just how Marx, Engels and Lassalle approached the analysis of concrete historical problems in individual countries. And a perusal of these instructive quotations from Marx and Engels reveals most strikingly the ridiculous position Rosa Luxemburg has placed herself in. She preaches eloquently and angrily the need for a concrete historical analysis of the national question in different countries at different times, but she *does not make the least* attempt to determine *what* historical stage in the development of capitalism *Russia* is passing through at the beginning of the twentieth century, or what the *specific features* of the national question in this country are. Rosa Luxemburg gives examples of how *others* have treated the question in a Marxist fashion, as if deliberately stressing how often the road to hell is paved with good intentions and how often good counsel covers up unwillingness or inability to follow such advice in practice.

Here is one of her edifying comparisons. In protesting against the demand for the independence of Poland, Rosa Luxemburg refers to a pamphlet she wrote in 1898, proving the rapid "industrial development of Poland", with the latter's manufactured goods being marketed in Russia. Needless to say, no conclusion whatever can be drawn from this on the question of the *right* to self-determination; it only proves the disappearance of the old Poland of the landed gentry, etc. But Rosa Luxemburg always passes on imperceptibly to the conclusion that among the factors that unite Russia and Poland, the purely economic factors of modern capitalist relations now predominate.

Then our Rosa proceeds to the question of autonomy, and though her article is entitled "The National Question and Autonomy" *in general*, she begins to argue that the Kingdom of Poland has an *exclusive* right to autonomy (see *Prosveshcheniye*, 1913, No. 12*). To support Poland's right to autonomy, Rosa Luxemburg evidently judges the state system of Russia by her economic, political and sociological characteristics and everyday life—a totality of features which, taken together, produce the concept of "Asiatic despotism". (*Przeglad*, No. 12, p. 137.)

It is generally known that this kind of state system possesses great stability whenever completely patriarchal and pre-capitalist features predominate in the economic system and where commodity production and class differen-

_____
* See this pamphlet, pp. 37-44.—*Ed.*

tiation are scarcely developed. However, if in a country whose state system is distinctly *pre*-capitalist in character there exists a nationally demarcated region where capitalism is *rapidly* developing, then the more rapidly that capitalism develops, the greater will be the antagonism between it and the *pre*-capitalist state system, and the more likely will be the separation of the progressive region from the whole— with which it is connected, not by "modern capitalistic", but by "Asiatically despotic" ties.

Thus, Rosa Luxemburg does not get her arguments to hang together even on the question of the social structure of the government in Russia with regard to bourgeois Poland; as for the concrete, historical, specific features of the national movements in Russia—she does not even raise that question.

That is a point we must now deal with.

3. The Concrete Features of the National Question in Russia, and Russia's Bourgeois-Democratic Reformation

"Despite the elasticity of the principle of 'the right of nations to self-determination', which is a mere platitude, and, obviously, equally applicable, not only to the nations inhabiting Russia, but also to the nations inhabiting Germany and Austria, Switzerland and Sweden, America and Australia, we do not find it in the programmes of any of the present-day socialist parties...." (*Przeglad* No. 6, p. 483.)

This is how Rosa Luxemburg opens her attack upon § 9 of the Marxist programme. In trying to foist on us the conception that this clause in the programme is a "mere platitude", Rosa Luxemburg herself falls victim to this error, alleging with amusing boldness that this point is, "obviously, equally applicable" to Russia, Germany, etc.

Obviously, we shall reply, Rosa Luxemburg has decided to make her article a collection of errors in logic that could be used for schoolboy exercises. For Rosa Luxemburg's tirade is sheer nonsense and a mockery of the historically concrete presentation of the question.

If one interprets the Marxist programme in Marxist fashion, not in a childish way, one will without difficulty grasp the fact that it refers to bourgeois-democratic national

54

movements. That being the case, it is "obvious" that this programme "sweepingly", and as a "mere platitude", etc., covers *all* instances of bourgeois-democratic national movements. No less obvious to Rosa Luxemburg, if she gave the slightest thought to it, would be the conclusion that our programme refers *only* to cases where such a movement is actually in existence.

Had she given thought to these obvious considerations, Rosa Luxemburg would have easily perceived what nonsense she was talking. In accusing *us* of uttering a "platitude" she has used *against us* the argument that no mention is made of the right to self-determination in the programmes of countries where there are *no* bourgeois-democratic national movements. A remarkably clever argument!

A comparison of the political and economic development of various countries, as well as of their Marxist programmes, is of tremendous importance from the standpoint of Marxism, for there can be no doubt that all modern states are of a common capitalist nature and are therefore subject to a common law of development. But such a comparison must be drawn in a sensible way. The elementary condition for comparison is to find out whether the historical periods of development of the countries concerned are at all *comparable*. For instance, only absolute ignoramuses (such as Prince Y. Trubetskoi in *Russkaya Mysl*[34]) are capable of "comparing" the Russian Marxists' agrarian programme with the programmes of Western Europe, since our programme replies to questions that concern the *bourgeois-democratic* agrarian reform, whereas in the Western countries no such question arises.

The same applies to the national question. In most Western countries it was settled long ago. It is ridiculous to seek an answer to non-existent questions in the programmes of Western Europe. In this respect Rosa Luxemburg has lost sight of the most important thing—the difference between countries where bourgeois-democratic reforms have long been completed, and those where they have not.

The crux of the matter lies in this difference. Rosa Luxemburg's complete disregard of it transforms her verbose article into a collection of empty and meaningless platitudes.

The epoch of bourgeois-democratic revolutions in Western, continental Europe embraces a fairly definite period, approximately between 1789 and 1871. This was precisely the period of national movements and the creation of national states. When this period drew to a close, Western Europe had been transformed into a settled system of bourgeois states, which, as a general rule, were nationally uniform states. Therefore, to seek the right to self-determination in the programmes of West-European socialists at this time of day is to betray one's ignorance of the ABC of Marxism.

In Eastern Europe and Asia the period of bourgeois-democratic revolutions did not begin until 1905. The revolutions in Russia, Persia, Turkey and China, the Balkan wars—such is the chain of world events of *our* period in our "Orient". And only a blind man could fail to see in this chain of events the awakening of a *whole series* of bourgeois-democratic national movements which strive to create nationally independent and nationally uniform states. It is precisely and solely because Russia and the neighbouring countries are passing through this period that we must have a clause in our programme on the right of nations to self-determination.

But let us continue the quotation from Rosa Luxemburg's article a little more. She writes:

"In particular, the programme of a party which is operating in a state with an extremely varied national composition, and for which the national question is a matter of first-rate importance—the programme of the Austrian Social-Democratic Party—does not contain the principle of the right of nations to self-determination." (Ibid.)

Thus, an attempt is made to convince the reader by the example of Austria "in particular". Let us examine this example in the light of concrete historical facts and see just how sound it is.

In the first place, let us pose the fundamental question of the completion of the bourgeois-democratic revolution. In Austria, this revolution began in 1848 and was over in 1867. Since then, a more or less fully established bourgeois constitution has dominated, for nearly half a century, and on its basis a legal workers' party is legally functioning.

Therefore, in the internal conditions of Austria's development (i.e., from the standpoint of the development of capitalism in Austria in general, and among its various nations in particular), there are *no* factors that produce leaps and bounds, a concomitant of which might be the formation of nationally independent states. In assuming, by her comparison, that Russia is in an analogous position in this respect, Rosa Luxemburg not only makes a fundamentally erroneous and anti-historical assumption, but also involuntarily slips into liquidationism.

Secondly, the profound difference in the relations between the nationalities in Austria and those in Russia is particularly important for the question we are concerned with. Not only was Austria for a long time a state in which the Germans preponderated, but the Austrian Germans laid claim to hegemony in the German nation as a whole. This "claim", as Rosa Luxemburg (who is seemingly so averse to commonplaces, platitudes, abstractions...) will perhaps be kind enough to remember, was shattered in the war of 1866. The German nation predominating in Austria found itself *outside the pale* of the independent German state which finally took shape in 1871. On the other hand, the Hungarians' attempt to create an independent national state collapsed under the blows of the Russian serf army as far back as 1849.

A very peculiar situation was thus created—a striving on the part of the Hungarians and then of the Czechs, not for separation from Austria, but, on the contrary, for the preservation of Austria's integrity, precisely in order to preserve national independence, which might have been completely crushed by more rapacious and powerful neighbours! Owing to this peculiar situation, Austria assumed the form of a dual state, and she is now being transformed into a triple state (Germans, Hungarians, Slavs).

Is there anything like this in Russia? Is there in our country a striving of the "subject peoples" for unity with the great Russians in face of the danger of *worse* national oppression?

One need only pose this question in order to see that the comparison between Russia and Austria on the question of self-determination of nations is meaningless, platitudinous and ignorant.

The peculiar conditions in Russia with regard to the national question are just the reverse of those we see in

Austria. Russia is a state with a single national centre—Great Russia. The Great Russians occupy a vast, unbroken stretch of territory, and number about 70,000,000. The specific features of this national state are: first, that "subject peoples" (which, on the whole, comprise the majority of the entire population—57 per cent) inhabit the border regions; secondly, the oppression of these subject peoples is much stronger here than in the neighbouring states (and not even in the European states alone); thirdly, in a number of cases the oppressed nationalities inhabiting the border regions have compatriots across the border, who enjoy greater national independence (suffice it to mention the Finns, the Swedes, the Poles, the Ukrainians and the Rumanians along the western and southern frontiers of the state); fourthly, the development of capitalism and the general level of culture are often higher in the non-Russian border regions than in the centre. Lastly, it is in the neighbouring Asian states that we see the beginning of a phase of bourgeois revolutions and national movements which are spreading to some of the kindred nationalities within the borders of Russia.

Thus, it is precisely the special concrete, historical features of the national question in Russia that make the recognition of the right of nations to self-determination in the present period a matter of special urgency in our country.

Incidentally, even from the purely factual angle, Rosa Luxemburg's assertion that the Austrian Social-Democrats' programme does not contain any recognition of the right of nations to self-determination is incorrect. We need only open the Minutes of the Brünn Congress, which adopted the national programme, to find the statements by the Ruthenian Social-Democrat Hankiewicz on behalf of the entire Ukrainian (Ruthenian) delegation (p. 85 of the Minutes), and by the Polish Social-Democrat Reger on behalf of the entire Polish delegation (p. 108), to the effect that one of the aspirations of the Austrian Social-Democrats of both the above-mentioned nations is to secure national unity, and the freedom and independence of their nations. Hence, while the Austrian Social-Democrats did not include the right of nations to self-determination directly in their programme, they did nevertheless allow the demand for national independence to be advanced by *sections* of the party. In effect, this means, of course, the recognition of the right of nations to self-determination! Thus, Rosa Luxemburg's reference to Austria speaks *against* Rosa Luxemburg in *all* respects.

4. "Practicality" in the National Question

Rosa Luxemburg's argument that § 9 of our Programme contains nothing "practical" has been seized upon by the opportunists. Rosa Luxemburg is so delighted with this argument that in some parts of her article this "slogan" is repeated eight times on a single page.

She writes: § 9 "gives no practical lead on the day-by-day policy of the proletariat, no practical solution of national problems".

Let us examine this argument, which elsewhere is formulated in such a way that it makes § 9 look quite meaningless, or else commits us to support all national aspirations.

What does the demand for "practicality" in the national question mean?

It means one of three things: support for all national aspirations; the answer "yes" or "no" to the question of secession by any nation; or that national demands are in general immediately "practicable".

Let us examine all three possible meanings of the demand for "practicality".

The bourgeoisie, which naturally assumes the leadership at the start of every national movement, says that support for all national aspirations is practical. However, the proletariat's policy in the national question (as in all others) supports the bourgeoisie only in a certain direction, but it never coincides with the bourgeoisie's policy. The working class supports the bourgeoisie only in order to secure national peace (which the bourgeoisie cannot bring about completely and which can be achieved only with *complete* democracy), in order to secure equal rights and to create the best conditions for the class struggle. Therefore, it is *in opposition to the practicality* of the bourgeoisie that the proletarians advance their *principles* in the national question; they always give the bourgeoisie *only conditional* support. What every bourgeoisie is out for in the national question is either privileges for its *own* nation, or exceptional advantages for it; this is called being "practical". The proletariat is opposed to all privileges, to all exclusiveness. To demand that it should be "practical" means following the lead of the bourgeoisie, falling into opportunism.

The demand for a "yes" or "no" reply to the question of secession in the case of every nation may seem a very "practical" one. In reality it is absurd; it is metaphysical in theory, while in practice it leads to subordinating the proletariat to the bourgeoisie's policy. The bourgeoisie always places its national demands in the forefront, and does so in categorical fashion. With the proletariat, however, these demands are subordinated to the interests of the class struggle. Theoretically, you cannot say in advance whether the bourgeois-democratic revolution will end in a given nation seceding from another nation, or in its equality with the latter; *in either case*, the important thing for the proletariat is to ensure the development of its class. For the bourgeoisie it is important to hamper this development by pushing the aims of its "own" nation before those of the proletariat. That is why the proletariat confines itself, so to speak, to the negative demand for recognition of the *right* to self-determination, without giving guarantees to any nation, and without undertaking to give *anything at the expense* of another nation.

This may not be "practical", but it is in effect the best guarantee for the achievement of the most democratic of all possible solutions. The proletariat needs *only* such guarantees, whereas the bourgeoisie of every nation requires guarantees for *its own* interest, regardless of the position of (or the possible disadvantages to) other nations.

The bourgeoisie is most of all interested in the "feasibility" of a given demand—hence the invariable policy of coming to terms with the bourgeoisie of other nations, to the detriment of the proletariat. For the proletariat, however, the important thing is to strengthen its class against the bourgeoisie and to educate the masses in the spirit of consistent democracy and socialism.

This may not be "practical" as far as the opportunists are concerned, but it is the only real guarantee, the right to a national state are possible and probable. We proletarians declare in advance that we are *opposed* to Great-Russian privileges, and this is what guides our entire propaganda and agitation.

In her quest for "practicality" Rosa Luxemburg has lost sight of the *principal* practical task both of the Great-Russian proletariat and of the proletariat of other nationalities: that of day-by-day agitation and propaganda against all state and national privileges, and for the right, the equal right of all nations, to their national state. This (at present) is our principal task in the national question, for only in this way can we defend the interests of democracy and the alliance of all proletarians of all nations on an equal footing.

This propaganda may be "unpractical" from the point of view of the Great-Russian oppressors, as well as from the point of view of the bourgeoisie of the oppressed nations (both demand a *definite* "yes" or "no", and accuse the Social-Democrats of being "vague"). In reality it is this propaganda, and this propaganda alone, that ensures the genuinely democratic, the genuinely socialist education of the masses. This is the only propaganda to ensure the greatest chances of national peace in Russia, should she remain a multinational state, and the most peaceful (and for the proletarian class struggle, harmless) division into separate national states, should the question of such a division arise.

To explain this policy—the only proletarian policy—in the national question more concretely, we shall examine the attitude of Great-Russian liberalism towards the "self-determination of nations", and the example of Norway's secession from Sweden.

5. The Liberal Bourgeoisie and the Socialist Opportunists in the National Question

We have seen that the following argument is one of Rosa Luxemburg's "trump cards" in her struggle against the programme of the Marxists in Russia: recognition of the right to self-determination is tantamount to supporting the bourgeois nationalism of the oppressed nations. On the

guarantee of the greater national equality and peace, despite the feudal landlords and the *nationalist* bourgeoisie.

The whole task of the proletarians in the national question is "unpractical" from the standpoint of the *nationalist* bourgeoisie of every nation, because the proletarians, opposed as they are to nationalism of every kind, demand "abstract" equality; they demand, as a matter of principle, that there should be no privileges, however slight. Failing to grasp this, Rosa Luxemburg, by her misguided eulogy of practicality, has opened the door wide for the opportunists, and especially for opportunist concessions to Great-Russian nationalism.

Why Great-Russian? Because the Great Russians in Russia are an oppressor nation, and opportunism in the national question will of course find expression among oppressed nations otherwise than among oppressor nations.

On the plea that its demands are "practical", the bourgeoisie of the oppressed nations will call upon the proletariat to support its aspirations unconditionally. The most practical procedure is to say a plain "yes" in favour of the secession of a *particular* nation rather than in favour of all nations having the *right* to secede!

The proletariat is opposed to such practicality. While recognising equality and equal rights to a national state, it values above all and places foremost the alliance of the proletarians of all nations, and assesses any national demand, any national separation, *from the angle* of the workers' class struggle. This call for practicality is in fact merely a call for uncritical acceptance of bourgeois aspirations.

By supporting the right to secession, we are told, you are supporting the bourgeois nationalism of the oppressed nations. This is what Rosa Luxemburg says, and she is echoed by Semkovsky, the opportunist, who incidentally is the only representative of liquidationist ideas on this question, in the liquidationist newspaper!

Our reply to this is: No, it is to the bourgeoisie that a "practical" solution of this question is important. To the workers the important thing is to distinguish the *principles* of the two trends. *Insofar as* the bourgeoisie of the oppressed nation fights the oppressor, we are always, in every case, and more strongly than anyone else, *in favour*, for we are the staunchest and the most consistent enemies of oppression. But insofar as the bourgeoisie of the oppressed nation stands for *its own* bourgeois nationalism, we stand against. We fight against the privileges and violence of the oppressor nation, and do not in any way condone strivings for privileges on the part of the oppressed nation.

If, in our political agitation, we fail to advance and advocate the slogan of the *right* to secession, we shall play into the hands, not only of the bourgeoisie, but also of the feudal landlords and the absolutism of the *oppressor* nation. Kautsky long ago used this argument against Rosa Luxemburg, and the argument is indisputable. When, in her anxiety not to "assist" the nationalist bourgeoisie of Poland, Rosa Luxemburg rejects the *right* to secession in the programme of the Marxists *in Russia*, she is *in fact* assisting the Great-Russian Black Hundreds. She is in fact assisting opportunist tolerance of the privileges (and worse than privileges) of the Great Russians.

Carried away by the struggle against nationalism in Poland, Rosa Luxemburg has forgotten the nationalism of the Great Russians, although it is *this* nationalism that is the most formidable at the present time. It is a nationalism that is more feudal than bourgeois, and is the principal obstacle to democracy and to the proletarian struggle. The bourgeois nationalism of *any* oppressed nation has a general democratic content that is directed *against* oppression, and it is this content that we *unconditionally* support. At the same time we strictly distinguish it from the tendency towards national exclusiveness; we fight against the tendency of the Polish bourgeois to oppress the Jews, etc., etc.

This is "unpractical" from the standpoint of the bourgeois and the philistine, but it is the only policy in the national question that is practical, based on principles, and really promotes democracy, liberty and proletarian unity.

The recognition of the right to secession for all; the appraisal of each concrete question of secession from the point of view of removing all inequality, all privileges, and all exclusiveness.

Let us consider the position of an oppressor nation. Can a nation be free if it oppresses other nations? It cannot.

The interests of the freedom of the Great-Russian population* require a struggle against such oppression. The long, centuries-old history of the suppression of the movements of the oppressed nations, and the systematic propaganda in favour of such suppression coming from the "upper" classes have created enormous obstacles to the cause of freedom of the Great-Russian people itself, in the form of prejudices, etc.

The Great-Russian Black Hundreds deliberately foster these prejudices and encourage them. The Great-Russian bourgeoisie tolerates or condones them. The Great-Russian proletariat cannot achieve *its own* aims or clear the road to its freedom without systematically countering these prejudices.

In Russia, the creation of an independent national state remains, for the time being, the privilege of the Great-Russian nation alone. We, the Great-Russian proletarians, who defend no privileges whatever, do not defend this privilege either. We are fighting on the ground of a definite state; we unite the workers of all nations living in this state; we cannot vouch for any particular path of national development, for we are marching to our class goal along *all* possible paths.

However, we cannot move towards that goal unless we combat all nationalism, and uphold the equality of the various nations. Whether the Ukraine, for example, is destined to form an independent state is a matter that will be determined by a thousand unpredictable factors. Without attempting idle "*guesses*", we firmly uphold something that is beyond doubt: the right of the Ukraine to form such a state. We respect this right; we do not uphold the privileges of Great Russians with regard to Ukrainians; we *educate* the masses in the spirit of recognition of that right, in the spirit of rejecting *state* privileges for any nation.

In the leaps which all nations have made in the period of bourgeois revolutions, clashes and struggles over the

---

* A certain L. Vl.[35] in Paris considers this word un-Marxist. This L. Vl. is amusingly "*superklug*" (too clever by half). And "this too-clever-by-half" L. Vl. apparently intends to write an essay on the deletion of the words "population", "nation", etc., from our minimum programme (having in mind the class struggle!).

other hand, she says, if we take this right to mean no more than combating all violence against other nations, there is no need for a special clause in the programme, for Social-Democrats are, in general, opposed to all national oppression and inequality.

The first argument, as Kautsky irrefutably proved nearly twenty years ago, is a case of blaming other people for one's own nationalism; in her fear of the nationalism of the bourgeoisie of oppressed nations, Rosa Luxemburg is *actually* playing into the hands of the Black-Hundred nationalism of the Great Russians! Her second argument is actually a timid evasion of the question whether or not recognition of national equality includes recognition of the right to secession. If it does, then Rosa Luxemburg admits that, in principle, § 9 of our Programme is correct. If it does not, then she does not recognise national equality. Shuffling and evasions will not help matters here!

However, the best way to test these and all similar arguments is to study the attitude of the *various classes* of society towards this question. For the Marxist this test is obligatory. We must proceed from what is objective; we must examine the relations between the classes on this point. In failing to do so, Rosa Luxemburg is guilty of those very sins of metaphysics, abstractions, platitudes, and sweeping statements, etc., of which she vainly tries to accuse her opponents.

We are discussing the Programme of the Marxists *in Russia*, i.e., of the Marxists of all the nationalities in Russia. Should we not examine the position of the *ruling* classes of Russia?

The position of the "bureaucracy" (we beg pardon for this inaccurate term) and of the feudal landlords of our united-nobility type is well known. They definitely reject both the equality of nationalities and the right to self-determination. Theirs is the old motto of the days of serfdom: autocracy, orthodoxy, and the national essence— the last term applying only to the Great-Russian nation. Even the Ukrainians are declared to be an "alien" people and their very language is being suppressed.

Let us glance at the Russian bourgeoisie, which was "called upon" to take part—a very modest part, it is true, but nevertheless some part—in the government, under the

"June Third"[36] legislative and administrative system. It will not need many words to prove that the Octobrists[37] are following the Rights in this question. Unfortunately, some Marxists pay much less attention to the stand of the Great-Russian liberal bourgeoisie, the Progressists and the Cadets.[38] Yet he who fails to study that stand and give it careful thought will inevitably flounder in abstractions and groundless statements in discussing the question of the right of nations to self-determination.

Skilled though it is in the art of diplomatically evading direct answers to "unpleasant" questions, *Rech*,[39] the principal organ of the Constitutional-Democratic Party, was compelled, in its controversy with *Pravda*[40] last year, to make certain valuable admissions. The trouble started over the All-Ukraine Students' Congress held in Lvov in the summer of 1913. Mr. Mogilyansky, the "Ukrainian expert" or Ukrainian correspondent of *Rech*, wrote an article in which he poured vitriolic abuse ("ravings", "adventurism", etc.) on the idea that the Ukraine should secede, an idea which Dontsov, a nationalist-socialist, had advocated and the above-mentioned congress approved.

While in no way identifying itself with Mr. Dontsov, and declaring explicitly that he was a nationalist-socialist and that many Ukrainian Marxists did not agree with him, *Rabochaya Pravda* stated that the *tone* of *Rech*, or, rather, the *way it formulated the question in principle*, was improper and reprehensible for a Great-Russian democrat, or for anyone desiring to pass as a democrat.* Let *Rech* repudiate the Dontsovs if it likes, but, *from the standpoint of principle*, a Great-Russian organ of democracy, which it claims to be, cannot be oblivious of the *freedom* to secede, the *right* to secede.

A few months later, *Rech*, No. 331, published an "explanation" from Mr. Mogilyansky, who had learned from the Ukrainian newspaper *Shlyakhi*,[41] published in Lvov, of Mr. Dontsov's reply, in which, incidentally, Dontsov stated that "the chauvinist attacks in *Rech* have been properly sullied [branded?] only in the Russian Social-Democratic press". This "explanation" consisted of the thrice-repeated statement that "criticism of Mr. Dontsov's recipes" "has nothing

---

* See V. I. Lenin, *Collected Works*, Vol. 19, pp. 268-69.—*Ed.*

in common with the repudiation of the right of nations to self-determination".

"It must be said," wrote Mr. Mogilyansky, "that even 'the right of nations to self-determination' is not a fetish [mark this!] beyond criticism: unwholesome conditions in the life of nations may give rise to unwholesome tendencies in national self-determination, and the fact that these are brought to light does not mean that the right of nations to self-determination has been rejected."

As you see, this liberal's talk of a "fetish" was quite in keeping with Rosa Luxemburg's. It was obvious that Mr. Mogilyansky was trying to evade a direct reply to the question whether or not he recognised the right to political self-determination, i.e., to secession.

The newspaper *Proletarskaya Pravda*, issue No. 4, for December 11, 1913, also put this question *point-blank* to Mr. Mogilyansky and to the Constitutional-Democratic *Party*.*

Thereupon *Rech* (No. 340) published an unsigned, i.e., official, editorial statement replying to this question. This reply boils down to the following three points:

1) §11 of the Constitutional-Democratic Party's programme speaks bluntly, precisely and clearly of the "right of nations to free *cultural* self-determination".

2) *Rech* affirms that *Proletarskaya Pravda* "hopelessly confuses" self-determination with separatism, with the secession of a given nation.

3) "*Actually, the Cadets have never pledged themselves to advocate the right of 'nations to secede' from the Russian state.*" (See the article "National-Liberalism and the Right of Nations to Self-Determination", in *Proletarskaya Pravda* No. 12, December 20, 1913.**)

Let us first consider the second point in the *Rech* statement. How strikingly it shows to the Semkovskys, Liebmans, Yurkeviches and other opportunists that the hue and cry they have raised about the alleged "vagueness", or "indefiniteness", of the term "self-determination" is *in fact*, i.e., from the standpoint of objective class relationships and the class struggle in Russia, *simply a rehash* of the liberal-monarchist bourgeoisie's utterances!

---

* Ibid., pp. 525-27.—*Ed.*
** Ibid., Vol. 20, pp. 56-58.—*Ed.*

Proletarskaya Pravda put the following *three* questions to the enlightened "Constitutional-Democratic" gentlemen of *Rech*: (1) do they deny that, throughout the entire history of international democracy, and especially since the middle of the nineteenth century, self-determination of nations has been understood to mean precisely political self-determination, the right to form an independent national state? (2) do they deny that the well-known resolution adopted by the International Socialist Congress in London in 1896 has the same meaning? and (3) do they deny that Plekhanov, in writing about self-determination as far back as 1902, meant precisely political self-determination? When *Proletarskaya Pravda* posed these three questions, *the Cadets fell silent!*

Not a word did they utter in reply, for they had nothing to say. They had to admit tacitly that *Proletarskaya Pravda* was absolutely right.

The liberals' outcries that the term "self-determination" is vague and that the Social-Democrats "hopelessly confuse" it with separatism are nothing more than attempts to *confuse* the issue, and evade recognition of a universally established democratic principle. If the Semkovskys, Liebmans and Yurkeviches were not so ignorant, they would be ashamed to address the workers in a *liberal* vein.

But to proceed. *Proletarskaya Pravda* compelled *Rech* to admit that, in the programme of the Constitutional-Democrats, the term "cultural" self-determination means in effect the *repudiation of political* self-determination.

"Actually, the Cadets have never pledged themselves to advocate the right of 'nations to secede' from the Russian state"—it was not without reason that *Proletarskaya Pravda* recommended to *Novoye Vremya* and *Zemshchina*[42] these words from *Rech* as an example of our Cadets' "loyalty". In its issue No. 13563, *Novoye Vremya*, which never, of course, misses an opportunity of mentioning "the Yids" and taking digs at the Cadets, nevertheless stated:

"What, to the Social-Democrats, is an axiom of political wisdom [i.e., recognition of the right of nations to self-determination, to secede], is today beginning to cause disagreement even among the Cadets."

By declaring that they "have never pledged themselves to advocate the right of nations to secede from the Russian state", the Cadets have, in principle, taken exactly the same stand as *Novoye Vremya*. This is precisely one of the fundamentals of Cadet *national-liberalism*, of their kinship with the Purishkeviches, and of their dependence, political, ideological and practical, on the latter. *Proletarskaya Pravda* wrote: "The Cadets have studied history and know only too well what—to put it mildly—pogrom-like actions the practice of the ancient right of the Purishkeviches to 'grab' 'em and hold 'em'[43] has often led to." Although perfectly aware of the feudalist source and nature of the Purishkeviches' omnipotence, the Cadets are, nevertheless, taking their stand *on the basis* of the relationships and frontiers created by that very class. Knowing full well that there is much in the relationships and frontiers created or fixed by this class that is un-European and anti-European (we would say Asiatic if this did not sound undeservedly slighting to the Japanese and Chinese), the Cadets, nevertheless, accept them as the utmost limit.

Thus, they are adjusting themselves to the Purishkeviches, cringing to them, fearing to jeopardise their position, protecting them from the people's movement, from the democracy. As *Proletarskaya Pravda* wrote: "In effect, this means adapting oneself to the interests of the feudal-minded landlords and to the worst nationalist prejudices of the dominant nation, instead of systematically combating those prejudices."

Being men who are familiar with history and claim to be democrats, the Cadets do not even attempt to assert that the democratic movement, which is today characteristic of both Eastern Europe and Asia and is striving to change both on the model of the civilised capitalist countries, is bound to leave intact the boundaries fixed by the feudal epoch, the epoch of the omnipotence of the Purishkeviches and the disfranchisement of wide strata of the bourgeoisie and petty bourgeoisie.

The fact that the question raised in the controversy between *Proletarskaya Pravda* and *Rech* was not merely a literary question, but one that involved a real political issue of the day, was proved, among other things, by the last conference of the Constitutional-Democratic Party held on March 23-25, 1914; in the official report of this conference in *Rech* (No. 83, of March 26, 1914) we read:

"A particularly lively discussion also took place on national problems. The Kiev deputies, who were supported by N. V. Nekrasov and A. M. Kolyubakin, pointed out that the national question was becoming a key issue, which would have to be faced up to more resolutely than hitherto. F. F. Kokoshkin pointed out, however [this "however" is like Shchedrin's "but"—"the ears never grow higher than the forehead, never!"] that both the programme and past political experience demanded that 'elastic formulas' of 'political self-determination of nationalities' should be handled very carefully."

This most remarkable line of reasoning at the Cadet conference deserves serious attention from all Marxists and all democrats. (We will note in parentheses that *Kievskaya Mysl*,[44] which is evidently very well informed and no doubt presents Mr. Kokoshkin's ideas correctly, added that, of course, as a warning to his opponents, he laid special stress on the danger of the "disintegration" of the state.)

The official report in *Rech* is composed with consummate diplomatic skill designed to lift the veil as little as possible and to conceal as much as possible. Yet, in the main, what took place at the Cadet conference is quite clear. The liberal-bourgeois delegates, who were familiar with the state of affairs in the Ukraine, and the "Left" Cadets raised the question *precisely of the political* self-determination of nations. Otherwise, there would have been no need for Mr. Kokoshkin to urge that this "formula" should be "handled carefully".

The Cadet programme, which was of course known to the delegates at the Cadet conference, speaks of "cultural", *not* of political self-determination. Hence, Mr. Kokoshkin was *defending* the programme *against* the Ukrainian delegates, and *against* the Left Cadets; he was defending "cultural" self-determination *as opposed to* "political" self-determination. It is perfectly clear that in opposing "political" self-determination, in playing up the danger of the "disintegration of the state", and in calling the formula "political self-determination" an "*elastic*" one (quite in keeping with Rosa Luxemburg!), Mr. Kokoshkin was defending Great-Russian national-liberalism against the more "Left" or more democratic elements of the Constitutional-Democratic Party and also against the Ukrainian bourgeoisie.

Mr. Kokoshkin won the day at the Cadet conference, as is evident from the treacherous little word "however" in the *Rech* report; Great-Russian national-liberalism has triumphed among the Cadets. Will not this victory help to clear the minds of those misguided individuals among the Marxists in Russia who, like the Cadets, have also begun to fear the "elastic formulas of political self-determination of nationalities"?

Let us, "however", examine the substance of Mr. Kokoshkin's line of thought. By referring to "past political experience" (i.e., evidently, the experience of 1905, when the Great-Russian bourgeoisie took alarm for its national privileges and scared the Cadet Party with its fears), and also by playing up the danger of the "disintegration of the state", Mr. Kokoshkin showed that he understood perfectly well that political self-determination can mean nothing else but the right to secede and form an independent national state. The question is—how should Mr. Kokoshkin's fears be appraised in the light of democracy in general, and the proletarian class struggle in particular?

Mr. Kokoshkin would have us believe that recognition of the right to secession increases the danger of the "disintegration of the state". This is the viewpoint of Constable Mymretsov,[45] whose motto was "grab 'em and hold 'em". From the viewpoint of democracy in general, the very opposite is the case: recognition of the right to secession *reduces* the danger of the "disintegration of the state".

Mr. Kokoshkin argues exactly like the nationalists do. At their last congress they attacked the Ukrainian "Mazeppists". The Ukrainian movement, Mr. Savenko and Co. exclaimed, threatens to weaken the ties between the Ukraine and Russia, since Austrian Ukrainophilism is strengthening the Ukrainians' ties with Austria! It remains unexplained why Russia cannot try to "strengthen" her ties with the Ukrainians *through the same method* that the Savenkos blame Austria for using, i.e., by granting the Ukrainians freedom to use their own language, self-government and an autonomous Diet.

The arguments of the Savenkos and Kokoshkins are exactly alike, and from the purely logical point of view they are equally ridiculous and absurd. Is it not clear that the more liberty the Ukrainian nationality enjoys in any particular country, the stronger its ties with that country will be? One would think that this truism could not be disputed without totally abandoning all the premises of democracy. Can there be greater freedom of nationality, as such, than the freedom to secede, the freedom to form an independent national state?

To clear up this question, which has been so confused by the liberals (and by those who are so misguided as to echo them), we shall cite a very simple example. Let us take the question of divorce. In her article Rosa Luxemburg writes that the centralised democratic state, while conceding autonomy to its constituent parts, should retain the most important branches of legislation, including legislation on divorce, under the jurisdiction of the central parliament. The concern that the central authority of the democratic state should retain the power to allow divorce can be readily understood. The reactionaries are opposed to freedom of divorce; they say that it must be "handled carefully" and loudly declare that it means the "disintegration of the family". The democrats, however, believe that the reactionaries are hypocrites, and that they are actually defending the omnipotence of the police and the bureaucracy, the privileges of one of the sexes, and the worst kind of oppression of women. They believe that in actual fact freedom of divorce will not cause the "disintegration" of family ties, but, on the contrary, will strengthen them on a democratic basis, which is the only possible and durable basis in civilised society.

To accuse those who support freedom of self-determination, i.e., freedom to secede, of encouraging separatism, is as foolish and hypocritical as accusing those who advocate freedom of divorce of encouraging the destruction of family ties. Just as in bourgeois society the defenders of privilege and corruption, on which bourgeois marriage rests, oppose freedom of divorce, so, in the capitalist state, repudiation of the right to self-determination, i.e., the right of nations to secede, means nothing more than defence of the privileges of the dominant nation and police methods of administration, to the detriment of democratic methods.

No doubt, the political chicanery arising from all the relationships existing in capitalist society sometimes leads members of parliament and journalists to indulge in frivolous and even nonsensical twaddle about one or another nation seceding. But only reactionaries can allow themselves to be frightened (or pretend to be frightened) by such talk. Those who stand by democratic principles, i.e., who insist that questions of state be decided by the mass of the population, know very well that there is a "tremendous distance"[46] between what the politicians prate about and what the people decide. From their daily experience the masses know perfectly well the value of geographical and economic ties and the advantages of a big market and a big state. They will, therefore, resort to secession only when national oppression and national friction make joint life absolutely intolerable and hinder any and all economic intercourse. In that case, the interests of capitalist development and of the freedom of the class struggle will be best served by secession.

Thus, from whatever angle we approach Mr. Kokoshkin's arguments, they prove to be the height of absurdity and a mockery of the principles of democracy. And yet there is a modicum of logic in these arguments, the logic of the class interests of the Great-Russian bourgeoisie. Like most members of the Constitutional-Democratic Party, Mr. Kokoshkin is a lackey of the money-bags of that bourgeoisie. He defends its privileges in general, and its *state* privileges in particular. He defends them hand in hand and shoulder to shoulder with Purishkevich, the only difference being that Purishkevich puts more faith in the feudalist cudgel, while Kokoshkin and Co. realise that this cudgel was badly damaged in 1905, and rely more on bourgeois methods of fooling the masses, such as frightening the petty bourgeoisie and the peasants with the spectre of the "disintegration of the state", and deluding them with phrases about blending "people's freedom" with historical tradition, etc.

The liberals' hostility to the principle of political self-determination of nations can have one, and only one, real class meaning: national-liberalism, defence of the state privileges of the Great-Russian bourgeoisie. And the opportunists among the Marxists in Russia, who today, under the Third of June regime, are against the right of nations to self-determination—the liquidator Semkovsky, the Bundist Liebman, the Ukrainian petty-bourgeois Yurkevich —are *actually* following in the wake of the national-liberals, and corrupting the working class with national-liberal ideas.

The interests of the working class and of its struggle against capitalism demand complete solidarity and the closest unity of the workers of all nations; they demand resistance to the nationalist policy of the bourgeoisie of every nationality. Hence, Social-Democrats would be deviating from proletarian policy and subordinating the workers to the policy of the bourgeoisie if they were to repudiate the right of nations to self-determination, i.e., the right of an oppressed nation to secede, or if they were to support all the national demands of the bourgeoisie of oppressed nations. It makes no difference to the hired worker whether he is exploited chiefly by the Great-Russian bourgeoisie rather than the non-Russian bourgeoisie, or by the Polish bourgeoisie rather than the Jewish bourgeoisie, etc. The hired worker who has come to understand his class interests is equally indifferent to the state privileges of the Great-Russian capitalists and to the promises of the Polish or Ukrainian capitalists to set up an earthly paradise when they obtain state privileges. Capitalism is developing and will continue to develop, anyway, both in integral states with a mixed population and in separate national states.

In any case the hired worker will be an object of exploitation. Successful struggle against exploitation requires that the proletariat be free of nationalism, and be absolutely neutral, so to speak, in the fight for supremacy that is going on among the bourgeoisie of the various nations. If the proletariat of any one nation gives the slightest support to the privileges of its "own" national bourgeoisie, that will inevitably rouse distrust among the proletariat of another nation; it will weaken the international class solidarity of the workers and divide them, to the delight of the bourgeoisie. Repudiation of the right to self-determination or to secession inevitably means, in practice, support for the privileges of the dominant nation.

We will get even more striking confirmation of this if we take the concrete case of Norway's secession from Sweden.

6. Norway's Secession from Sweden

Rosa Luxemburg cites precisely this example, and discusses it as follows:

"The latest event in the history of federative relations, the secession of Norway from Sweden—which at the time was hastily seized upon

74

by the social-patriotic Polish press (see the Cracow *Naprzód*[47]) as a gratifying sign of the strength and progressive nature of the tendency towards state secession—at once provided striking proof that federalism and its concomitant, separation, are in no way an expression of progress or democracy. After the so-called Norwegian 'revolution', which meant that the Swedish king was deposed and compelled to leave Norway, the Norwegians coolly proceeded to choose another king, formally rejecting, by a national referendum, the proposal to establish a republic. That which superficial admirers of all national movements and of all semblance of independence proclaimed to be a 'revolution' was simply a manifestation of peasant and petty-bourgeois particularism, the desire to have a king 'of their own' for their money instead of one imposed upon them by the Swedish aristocracy, and was, consequently, a movement that had absolutely nothing in common with revolution. At the same time, the dissolution of the union between Sweden and Norway showed once more to what extent, in this case also, the federation which had existed until then was only an expression of purely dynastic interests and, therefore, merely a form of monarchism and reaction." (*Przeglad.*)

That is literally all that Rosa Luxemburg has to say on this score! Admittedly, it would have been difficult for her to have revealed the hopelessness of her position more saliently than she has done in this particular instance.

The question was, and is: do the Social-Democrats in a mixed national state need a programme that recognises the right to self-determination or secession?

What does the example of Norway, cited by Rosa Luxemburg, tell us on this point?

Our author twists and turns, exercises her wit and rails at *Naprzód*, but she does not answer the question! Rosa Luxemburg speaks about everything under the sun so as to *avoid saying a single word* about the actual point at issue!

Undoubtedly, in wishing to have a king of their own for their money, and in rejecting, in a national referendum, the proposal to establish a republic, the Norwegian petty bourgeoisie displayed exceedingly bad philistine qualities. Undoubtedly, *Naprzód* displayed equally bad and equally philistine qualities in failing to notice this.

But what has all this to do with the case?

The question under discussion was the right of nations to self-determination and the attitude to be adopted by the socialist proletariat towards this right! Why, then, does not Rosa Luxemburg answer this question instead of beating about the bush?

To a mouse there is no stronger beast than the cat, it is said. To Rosa Luxemburg there is evidently no stronger beast than the "Fracy". "Fracy" is the popular term for the "Polish Socialist Party", its so-called revolutionary section, and the Cracow newspaper *Naprzód* shares the views of that "section". Rosa Luxemburg is so blinded by her fight against the nationalism of that "section" that she loses sight of everything except *Naprzód*.

If *Naprzód* says "yes", Rosa Luxemburg considers it her sacred duty to say an immediate "no", without stopping to think that by so doing she does not reveal independence of *Naprzód*, but, on the contrary, her ludicrous dependence on the "Fracy" and her inability to see things from a viewpoint any deeper and broader than that of the Cracow anthill. *Naprzód*, of course, is a wretched and by no means Marxist organ; but that should not prevent us from properly analysing the example of Norway, once we have chosen it.

To analyse this example in Marxist fashion, we must deal, not with the vices of the awfully terrible "Fracy", but, first, with the concrete historical features of the secession of Norway from Sweden, and secondly, with the tasks which confronted the *proletariat* of both countries in connection with this secession.

The geographic, economic and language ties between Norway and Sweden are as intimate as those between the Great Russians and many other Slav nations. But the union between Norway and Sweden was not a voluntary one, and in dragging in the question of "federation" Rosa Luxemburg was talking at random, simply because she did not know what to say. Norway was *ceded* to Sweden by the monarchs during the Napoleonic wars, against the will of the Norwegians; and the Swedes had to bring troops into Norway to subdue her.

Despite the very extensive autonomy which Norway enjoyed (she had her own parliament, etc.), there was constant friction between Norway and Sweden for many decades after the union, and the Norwegians strove hard to throw off the yoke of the Swedish aristocracy. At last, in August 1905, they succeeded: the Norwegian parliament resolved that the Swedish king was no longer king of Norway, and in the referendum held later among the Norwegian people, the overwhelming majority (about 200,000 as against a few hundred) voted for complete separation from Sweden. After a short period of indecision, the Swedes resigned themselves to the fact of secession.

This example shows us on what grounds cases of the secession of nations are practicable, and actually occur, under modern economic and political relationships, and the *form* secession sometimes assumes under conditions of political freedom and democracy.

No Social-Democrat will deny—unless he would profess indifference to questions of political freedom and democracy (in which case he is naturally no longer a Social-Democrat)—that this example *virtually* proves that it is the *bounden duty* of class-conscious workers to conduct systematic propaganda and prepare the ground for the settlement of conflicts that may arise over the secession of nations, not in the "Russian way", but *only in the way* they were settled in 1905 between Norway and Sweden. This is exactly what is meant by the demand in the programme for the recognition of the right of nations to self-determination. But Rosa Luxemburg tried to get around a fact that was repugnant to her theory by violently attacking the philistinism of the Norwegian philistines and the Cracow *Naprzód*; for she understood perfectly well that this historical fact *completely refutes* her phrases about the right of nations to self-determination being a "utopia", or like the right "to eat off gold plates", etc. Such phrases only express a smug and opportunist belief in the immutability of the present alignment of forces among the nationalities of Eastern Europe.

To proceed. In the question of the self-determination of nations, as in every other question, we are interested first and foremost, in the self-determination of the proletariat within a given nation. Rosa Luxemburg modestly evaded this question too, for she realised that an analysis of it on the basis of the example of Norway, which she herself had chosen, would be disastrous to her "theory".

What position did the Norwegian and Swedish proletariat take, and indeed had to take, in the conflict over secession? *After* Norway seceded, the class-conscious workers

77

of Norway would naturally have voted for a republic,* and if some socialists voted otherwise it only goes to show how much dense, philistine opportunism there sometimes is in the European socialist movement. There can be no two opinions about that, and we mention the point only because Rosa Luxemburg is trying to obscure the issue by speaking *off the mark*. We do not know whether the Norwegian socialist programme made it obligatory for Norwegian Social-Democrats to hold particular views on the question of secession. We will assume that it did not, and that the Norwegian socialists left it an open question as to what extent the autonomy of Norway gave sufficient scope to wage the class struggle freely, or to what extent the eternal friction and conflicts with the Swedish aristocracy hindered freedom of economic life. But it cannot be disputed that the Norwegian proletariat had to oppose this aristocracy and support Norwegian peasant democracy (with all its philistine limitations).

And the Swedish proletariat? It is common knowledge that the Swedish landed proprietors, abetted by the Swedish clergy, advocated war against Norway. Inasmuch as Norway was much weaker than Sweden, had already experienced a Swedish invasion, and the Swedish aristocracy carries enormous weight in its own country, this advocacy of war presented a grave danger. We may be sure that the Swedish Kokoshkins spent much time and energy in trying to corrupt the minds of the Swedish people by appeals to "handle" the "elastic formulas of political self-determination of nations carefully", by painting horrific pictures of the danger of the "disintegration of the state" and by assuring them that "people's freedom" was compatible with the traditions of the Swedish aristocracy. There cannot be the slightest doubt that the Swedish Social-Democrats would have betrayed the cause of socialism and democracy if they had not fought with all their might to combat both the landlord and the "Kokoshkin" ideology and policy, and if they had failed to demand, *not only* equality of nations

---

* Since the majority of the Norwegian nation was in favour of a monarchy while the proletariat wanted a republic, the Norwegian proletariat was, generally speaking, confronted with the alternative: either revolution, if conditions were ripe for it, or submission to the will of the majority and prolonged propaganda and agitation work.

in general (to which the Kokoshkins also subscribe), but also the right of nations to self-determination, Norway's freedom to secede.

The close alliance between the Norwegian and Swedish workers, their complete fraternal class solidarity, *gained* from the Swedish workers' recognition of the right of the Norwegians to secede. This convinced the Norwegian workers that the Swedish workers were not infected with Swedish nationalism, and that they placed fraternity with the Norwegian proletarians above the privileges of the Swedish bourgeoisie and aristocracy. The dissolution of the ties imposed upon Norway by the monarchs of Europe and the Swedish aristocracy strengthened the ties between the Norwegian and Swedish workers. The Swedish workers have proved that in spite of *all* the vicissitudes of bourgeois policy—bourgeois relations may quite possibly bring about a repetition of the forcible subjection of the Norwegians to the Swedes!—they will be able to preserve and defend the complete equality and class solidarity of the workers of both nations in the struggle against both the Swedish and the Norwegian bourgeoisie.

Incidentally, this reveals how groundless and even frivolous are the attempts sometimes made by the "Fracy" to "use" our disagreements with Rosa Luxemburg against Polish Social-Democracy. The "Fracy" are not a proletarian or a socialist party, but a petty-bourgeois nationalist party, something like Polish Social-Revolutionaries. There never has been, nor could there be, any question of unity between the Russian Social-Democrats and this party. On the other hand, no Russian Social-Democrat has ever "repented" of the close relations and unity that have been established with the Polish Social-Democrats. The Polish Social-Democrats have rendered a great historical service by creating the first really Marxist, proletarian party in Poland, a country imbued with nationalist aspirations and passions. Yet the service the Polish Social-Democrats have rendered is a great one, not because Rosa Luxemburg has talked a lot of nonsense about § 9 of the Russian Marxists' Programme, but despite that sad circumstance.

The question of the "right to self-determination" is of course not so important to the Polish Social-Democrats as it is to the Russian. It is quite understandable that in their zeal (sometimes a little excessive, perhaps) to combat the nationalistically blinded petty bourgeoisie of Poland the Polish Social-Democrats should overdo things. No Russian Marxist has ever thought of blaming the Polish Social-Democrats for being opposed to the secession of Poland. These Social-Democrats err only when, like Rosa Luxemburg, they try to deny the necessity of including the recognition of the right to self-determination in the Programme of the *Russian* Marxists.

Virtually, this is like attempting to apply relationships, understandable by Cracow standards, to all the peoples and nations inhabiting Russia, including the Great Russians. It means being "Polish nationalists the wrong way round", not Russian, not international Social-Democrats.

For international Social-Democracy stands for the recognition of the right of nations to self-determination. This is what we shall now proceed to discuss.

7. The Resolution of the London International Congress, 1896

This resolution reads:

"This Congress declares that it stands for the full right of all nations to self-determination [*Selbstbestimmungsrecht*] and expresses its sympathy for the workers of every country now suffering under the yoke of military, national or other absolutism. This Congress calls upon the workers of all these countries to join the ranks of the class-conscious [*Klassenbewusste*—those who understand their class interests] workers of the whole world in order jointly to fight for the defeat of international capitalism and for the achievement of the aims of international Social-Democracy."*

As we have already pointed out, our opportunists— Semkovsky, Liebman and Yurkevich—are simply unaware of this resolution. But Rosa Luxemburg knows it and

---

* See the official German report of the London Congress: *Verhandlungen und Beschlüsse des internationalen sozialistischen Arbeiter- und Gewerkschafts-Kongresses zu London, vom 27. Juli bis 1. August 1896*, Berlin, 1897, S. 18. A Russian pamphlet has been published containing the decisions of international congresses in which the word "self-determination" is wrongly translated as "autonomy".

quotes the full text, which contains the same expression as that contained in our programme, viz., "self-determination".

How does Rosa Luxemburg remove this obstacle from the path of her "original" theory?

Oh, quite simply ... the whole emphasis lies in the second part of the resolution ... its declarative character ... one can refer to it only by mistake!

The feebleness and utter confusion of our author are simply amazing. Usually it is only the opportunists who talk about the consistent democratic and socialist points in the programme being mere declarations, and cravenly avoid an open debate on them. It is apparently not without reason that Rosa Luxemburg has this time found herself in the deplorable company of the Semkovskys, Liebmans and Yurkeviches. Rosa Luxemburg does not venture to state openly whether she regards the above resolution as correct or erroneous. She shifts and shuffles as if counting on the inattentive or ill-informed reader, who forgets the first part of the resolution by the time he has started reading the second, or who has never heard of the discussion that took place in the socialist press *prior* to the London Congress.

Rosa Luxemburg is greatly mistaken, however, if she imagines that, in the sight of the class-conscious workers of Russia, she can get away with trampling upon the resolution of the International on such an important, fundamental issue, without even deigning to analyse it critically.

Rosa Luxemburg's point of view was voiced during the discussions which took place prior to the London Congress, mainly in the columns of *Die Neue Zeit*, organ of the German Marxists; *in essence this point of view was defeated in the International*! That is the crux of the matter, which the Russian reader must particularly bear in mind.

The debate turned on the question of Poland's independence. Three points of view were put forward:

1. That of the "Fracy", in whose name Haecker spoke. They wanted the International to include in *its own* programme a demand for the independence of Poland. The

motion was not carried and this point of view was defeated in the International.

2. Rosa Luxemburg's point of view, viz., the Polish socialists should not demand independence for Poland. This point of view entirely precluded the proclamation of the right of nations to self-determination. It was likewise defeated in the International.

3. The point of view which was elaborated at the time by K. Kautsky, who opposed Rosa Luxemburg and proved that her materialism was extremely "one-sided"; according to Kautsky, the International could not at the time make the independence of Poland a point in its programme; but the Polish socialists were fully entitled to put forward such a demand. From the socialists' point of view it was undoubtedly a mistake to ignore the tasks of national liberation in a situation where national oppression existed.

The International's resolution reproduces the most essential and fundamental propositions in this point of view: on the one hand, the absolutely direct, unequivocal recognition of the full right of all nations to self-determination; on the other hand, the equally unambiguous appeal to the workers for *international* unity in their class struggle.

We think that this resolution is absolutely correct, and that, to the countries of Eastern Europe and Asia at the beginning of the twentieth century, it is this resolution, with both its parts being taken as an integral whole, that gives the only correct lead to the proletarian class policy in the national question.

Let us deal with the three above-mentioned viewpoints in somewhat greater detail.

As is known, Karl Marx and Frederick Engels considered it the bounden duty of the whole of West-European democracy, and still more of Social-Democracy, to give active support to the demand for Polish independence. For the period of the 1840s and 1860s, the period of the bourgeois revolutions in Austria and Germany, and the period of the "Peasant Reform" in Russia, this point of view was quite correct and the only one that was consistently democratic and proletarian. So long as the masses of the people in Russia and in most of the Slav countries were still sunk in torpor, so long as *there were no* independent, mass, democratic movements in those countries, the liberation movement of the *gentry* in Poland assumed an immense and paramount importance from the point of view, not only of Russian, not only of Slav, but of European democracy as a whole.*

But while Marx's standpoint was quite correct for the forties, fifties and sixties or for the third quarter of the nineteenth century, it has ceased to be correct by the twentieth century. Independent democratic movements, and even an independent proletarian movement, have arisen in most Slav countries, even in Russia, one of the most backward Slav countries. Aristocratic Poland has disappeared, yielding place to capitalist Poland. Under such circumstances Poland could not but lose her *exceptional* revolutionary importance.

The attempt of the P.S.P. (the Polish Socialist Party, the present-day "Fracy") in 1896 to "establish" for all time the point of view Marx had held in a *different epoch* was an attempt to use the *letter* of Marxism against the *spirit* of Marxism. The Polish Social-Democrats were therefore quite right in attacking the extreme nationalism of the Polish petty bourgeoisie and pointing out that the national question was of secondary importance to Polish workers, in creating for the first time a purely proletarian party in Poland and proclaiming the extremely important principle that the Polish and the Russian workers must maintain the closest alliance in their class struggle.

But did this mean that at the beginning of the twentieth century the International could regard the principle of political self-determination of nations, or the right to secede,

---

* It would be a very interesting piece of historical research to compare the position of a noble Polish rebel in 1863 with that of the all-Russia revolutionary democrat, Chernyshevsky, who (like Marx) was able to appreciate the importance of the Polish movement, and with that of the Ukrainian petty bourgeois Dragomanov, who appeared much later and expressed the views of a peasant, so ignorant and sluggish, and so attached to his dung heap, that his legitimate hatred of the Polish gentry blinded him to the significance which their struggle had for all-Russia democracy. (Cf. Dragomanov, *Historical Poland and Great-Russian Democracy*.) Dragomanov richly deserved the fervent kisses which were subsequently bestowed on him by Mr. P. B. Struve, who by that time had become a national-liberal.

as unnecessary to Eastern Europe and Asia? This would have been the height of absurdity, and (theoretically) tantamount to admitting that the bourgeois-democratic reform of the Turkish, Russian and Chinese states had been consummated; indeed it would have been tantamount (in practice) to opportunism towards absolutism.

No. At a time when bourgeois-democratic revolutions in Eastern Europe and Asia have begun, in this period of the awakening and intensification of national movements and of the formation of independent proletarian parties, the task of these parties with regard to national policy must be twofold: recognition of the right of all nations to self-determination, since bourgeois-democratic reform is not yet completed and since working-class democracy consistently, seriously and sincerely (and not in a liberal, Kokoshkin fashion) fights for equal rights for nations; then, a close, unbreakable alliance in the class struggle of the proletarians of all nations in a given state, throughout all the changes in its history, irrespective of any reshaping of the frontiers of the individual states by the bourgeoisie.

It is this twofold task of the proletariat that the 1896 resolution of the International formulates. That is the substance, the underlying principle, of the resolution adopted by the Conference of Russian Marxists held in the summer of 1913. Some people profess to see a "contradiction" in the fact that while point 4 of this resolution, which recognises the right to self-determination and secession, seems to "concede" the maximum to nationalism (in reality, the recognition of the *right of all* nations to self-determination implies the maximum of *democracy* and the minimum of nationalism), point 5 warns the workers against the nationalist slogans of the bourgeoisie of any nation and demands the unity and amalgamation of the workers of all nations in internationally united proletarian organisations. But this is a "contradiction" only for extremely shallow minds, which, for instance, cannot grasp why the unity and class solidarity of the Swedish and the Norwegian proletariat *gained* when the Swedish workers upheld Norway's freedom to secede and form an independent state.

8. The Utopian Karl Marx and the Practical Rosa Luxemburg

Calling Polish independence a "utopia" and repeating this *ad nauseam*, Rosa Luxemburg exclaims ironically: Why not raise the demand for the independence of Ireland?

The "practical" Rosa Luxemburg evidently does not know what Karl Marx's attitude to the question of Irish independence was. It is worth while dwelling upon this, so as to show how a *concrete* demand for national independence was analysed from a genuinely Marxist, not opportunist, standpoint.

It was Marx's custom to "sound out" his socialist acquaintances, as he expressed it, to test their intelligence and the strength of their convictions.[48] After making the acquaintance of Lopatin, Marx wrote to Engels on July 5, 1870, expressing a highly flattering opinion of the young Russian socialist but adding at the same time:

"*Poland* is his weak point. On this point he speaks quite like an Englishman—say, an English Chartist of the old school—about Ireland."[49]

Marx questions a socialist belonging to an oppressor nation about his attitude to the oppressed nation and at once reveals a defect *common* to the socialists of the dominant nations (the English and the Russian): failure to understand their socialist duties towards the downtrodden nations, their echoing of the prejudices acquired from the bourgeoisie of the "dominant nation".

Before passing on to Marx's positive declarations on Ireland, we must point out that in general the attitude of Marx and Engels to the national question was strictly critical, and that they recognised its historically conditioned importance. Thus, Engels wrote to Marx on May 23, 1851, that the study of history was leading him to pessimistic conclusions in regard to Poland, that the importance of Poland was temporary—only until the agrarian revolution in Russia. The role of the Poles in history was one of "bold (hotheaded) foolishness". "And one cannot point to a single instance in which Poland has successfully represented progress, even in relation to Russia, or done anything at all of historical importance." Russia contains more of civilisation, education, industry and the bourgeoisie than "the Poland of the indolent gentry". "What are Warsaw and Cracow compared to St. Petersburg, Moscow, Odessa!" Engels had no faith in the success of the Polish gentry's insurrections.

But all these thoughts, showing the deep insight of genius, by no means prevented Engels and Marx from treating the Polish movement with the most profound and ardent sympathy twelve years later, when Russia was still dormant and Poland was seething.

When drafting the Address of the International in 1864, Marx wrote to Engels (on November 4, 1864) that he had to combat Mazzini's nationalism, and went on to say: "Inasmuch as international politics occurred in the Address, I spoke of countries, not of nationalities, and denounced Russia, not the *minores gentium*." Marx had no doubt as to the subordinate position of the national question as compared with the "labour question". But his theory is as far from ignoring national movements as heaven is from earth.

Then came 1866. Marx wrote to Engels about the "Proudhonist clique" in Paris which "declares nationalities to be an absurdity, attacks Bismarck and Garibaldi. As polemics against chauvinism their doings are useful and explicable. But as believers in Proudhon (Lafargue and Longuet, two very good friends of mine here, also belong to them), who think all Europe must and will sit quietly on their hind quarters until the gentlemen in France abolish poverty and ignorance—they are grotesque." (Letter of June 7, 1866.)

"Yesterday," Marx wrote on June 20, 1866, "there was a discussion in the International Council on the present war.... The discussion wound up, as was to be foreseen, with 'the question of nationality' in general and the attitude we take towards it.... The representatives of 'Young France' (*non-workers*) came out with the announcement that all nationalities and even nations were 'antiquated prejudices'. Proudhonised Stirnerism.... The whole world waits until the French are ripe for a social revolution.... The English laughed very much when I began my speech by saying that our friend Lafargue and others, who had done away with nationalities, had spoken 'French' to us, i.e., a language which nine-tenths of the audience did not understand. I also suggested that by the negation of nationalities he appeared, quite unconsciously, to understand their absorption by the model French nation."[50]

The conclusion that follows from all these critical remarks of Marx's is clear: the working class should be the last to make a fetish of the national question, since the development of capitalism does not necessarily awaken *all* nations to independent life. But to brush aside the mass national movements once they have started, and to refuse to support what is progressive in them means, in effect, pandering to *nationalistic* prejudices, that is, recognising "one's own nation" as a model nation (or, we would add, one possessing the exclusive privilege of forming a state).*

But let us return to the question of Ireland.

Marx's position on this question is most clearly expressed in the following extracts from his letters:

"I have done my best to bring about this demonstration of the English workers in favour of Fenianism.... I used to think the separation of Ireland from England impossible. I now think it inevitable, although after the separation there may come federation." This is what Marx wrote to Engels on November 2, 1867.

In his letter of November 30 of the same year he added:

"...what shall we advise the *English* workers? In my opinion they must make the *Repeal of the Union* [Ireland with England, i.e., the separation of Ireland from England] (in short, the affair of 1783, only democratised and adapted to the conditions of the time) an article of their *pronunziamento*. This is the only legal and therefore only possible form of Irish emancipation which can be admitted in the programme of an *English* party. Experience must show later whether a mere personal union can continue to subsist between the two countries....

"...What the Irish need is:

"1) Self-government and independence from England;

"2) An agrarian revolution...."

---

* Cf. also Marx's letter to Engels of June 3, 1867: "... I have learned with real pleasure from the Paris letters to *The Times* about the pro-Polish exclamations of the Parisians against Russia.... Mr. Proudhon and his little doctrinaire clique are not the French people."

Marx attached great importance to the Irish question and delivered hour-and-a-half lectures on this subject at the German Workers' Union (letter of December 17, 1867).[51]

In a letter dated November 20, 1868, Engels spoke of "the hatred towards the Irish found among the English workers", and almost a year later (October 24, 1869), returning to this subject, he wrote:

"*Il n'y a qu'un pas* [it is only one step] from Ireland to Russia.... Irish history shows what a misfortune it is for one nation to have subjugated another. All the abominations of the English have their origin in the Irish Pale. I have still to plough my way through the Cromwellian period, but this much seems certain to me, that things would have taken another turn in England, too, but for the necessity of military rule in Ireland and the creation of a new aristocracy there."

Let us note, in passing, Marx's letter to Engels of August 18, 1869:

"The Polish workers in Posen have brought a strike to a victorious end with the help of their colleagues in Berlin. This struggle against Monsieur le Capital—even in the lower form of the strike—is a more serious way of getting rid of national prejudices than peace declamations from the lips of bourgeois gentlemen."

The policy on the Irish question pursued by Marx in the International may be seen from the following:

On November 18, 1869, Marx wrote to Engels that he had spoken for an hour and a quarter at the Council of the International on the question of the attitude of the British Ministry to the Irish Amnesty, and had proposed the following resolution:

"Resolved,

"that in his reply to the Irish demands for the release of the imprisoned Irish patriots Mr. Gladstone deliberately insults the Irish nation;

"that he clogs political amnesty with conditions alike degrading to the victims of misgovernment and the people they belong to;

"that having, in the teeth of his responsible position, publicly and enthusiastically cheered on the American slaveholders' rebellion, he now steps in to preach to the Irish people the doctrine of passive obedience;

"that his whole proceedings with reference to the Irish Amnesty question are the true and genuine offspring of that '*policy of conquest*', by the fiery denunciation of which Mr. Gladstone ousted his Tory rivals from office;

"that the General Council of the International Workingmen's Association express their admiration of the spirited, firm and high-souled manner in which the Irish people carry on their Amnesty movement;

"that this resolution be communicated to all branches of, and workingmen's bodies connected with, the International Workingmen's Association in Europe and America."

On December 10, 1869, Marx wrote that his paper on the Irish question to be read at the Council of the International would be couched as follows:

"Quite apart from all phrases about 'international' and 'humane' justice for Ireland—which are taken for granted in the International Council—*it is in the direct and absolute interest of the English working class to get rid of their present connexion with Ireland*. And this is my fullest conviction, and for reasons which in part I can *not* tell the English workers themselves. For a long time I believed that it would be possible to overthrow the Irish regime by English working-class ascendancy. I always expressed this point of view in the *New York Tribune* [an American paper to which Marx contributed for a long time]. Deeper study has now convinced me of the opposite. The English working class will *never accomplish anything* until it has got rid of Ireland. ... The English reaction in England had its roots in the subjugation of Ireland." (Marx's italics.)[52]

Marx's policy on the Irish question should now be quite clear to our readers.

Marx, the "utopian", was so "unpractical" that he stood for the separation of Ireland, which half a century later has not yet been achieved.

What gave rise to Marx's policy, and was it not mistaken?

At first Marx thought that Ireland would not be liberated by the national movement of the oppressed nation, but by the working-class movement of the oppressor nation. Marx did not make an Absolute of the national movement, knowing, as he did, that only the victory of the working class can bring about the complete liberation of all nationalities. It is impossible to estimate beforehand all the possible relations between the bourgeois liberation movements of the oppressed nations and the proletarian emancipation movement of the oppressor nation (the very problem which today makes the national question in Russia so difficult).

However, it so happened that the English working class fell under the influence of the Liberals for a fairly long time, became an appendage to the Liberals, and by adopting a liberal-labour policy left itself leaderless. The bourgeois liberation movement in Ireland grew stronger and assumed revolutionary forms. Marx reconsidered his view and corrected it. "What a misfortune it is for a nation to have subjugated another." The English working class will never be free until Ireland is freed from the English yoke. Reaction in England is strengthened and fostered by the enslavement of Ireland (just as reaction in Russia is fostered by her enslavement of a number of nations!).

And, in proposing in the International a resolution of sympathy with "the Irish nation", "the Irish people" (the clever L.Vl. would probably have berated poor Marx for forgetting about the class struggle!), Marx advocated the *separation* of Ireland from England, "although after the separation there may come federation".

What were the theoretical grounds for Marx's conclusion? In England the bourgeois revolution had been consummated long ago. But it had not yet been consummated in Ireland; it is being consummated only now, after the lapse of half a century, by the reforms of the English Liberals. If capitalism had been overthrown in England as quickly as Marx had at first expected, there would have been no room for a bourgeois-democratic and general national movement in Ireland. But since it had arisen, Marx advised the English workers to support it, give it a revolutionary impetus and see it through in the interests of *their own* liberty.

The economic ties between Ireland and England in the 1860s were, of course, even closer than Russia's present ties with Poland, the Ukraine, etc. The "unpracticality" and "impracticability" of the separation of Ireland (if only owing to geographical conditions and England's immense colonial power) were quite obvious. Though, in principle, an enemy of federalism, Marx in this instance granted the possibility of federation, as well,* *if only* the emancipation of Ireland was achieved in a revolutionary, not reformist way, through a movement of the mass of the people of Ireland supported by the working class of England. There can be no doubt that only such a solution of the historical problem would have been in the best interests of the proletariat and most conducive to rapid social progress.

Things turned out differently. Both the Irish people and the English proletariat proved weak. Only now, through the sordid deals between the English Liberals and the Irish bourgeoisie, is the Irish problem *being solved* (the example of Ulster shows with what difficulty) through the land reform (with compensation) and Home Rule (not yet introduced). Well then? Does it follow that Marx and Engels were "utopians", that they put forward "impracticable" national demands, or that they allowed themselves to be influenced by the Irish petty-bourgeois nationalists (for there is no doubt about the petty-bourgeois nature of the Fenian movement), etc.?

No. In the Irish question, too, Marx and Engels pursued a consistently proletarian policy, which really educated the masses in a spirit of democracy and socialism. Only such a policy could have saved both Ireland and England half a century of delay in introducing the necessary reforms, and prevented these reforms from being mutilated by the Liberals to please the reactionaries.

The policy of Marx and Engels on the Irish question serves as a splendid example of the attitude the proletariat of the oppressor nations should adopt towards national

---

* By the way, it is not difficult to see why, from a Social-Democratic point of view, the right to "self-determination" means *neither* federation *nor* autonomy (although, speaking in the abstract, both come under the category of "self-determination"). The right to federation is simply meaningless, since federation implies a bilateral contract. It goes without saying that Marxists cannot include the defence of federalism in general in their programme. As far as autonomy is concerned, Marxists defend, not the "right" to autonomy, but autonomy *itself*, as a general universal principle of a democratic state with a mixed national composition, and a great variety of geographical and other conditions. Consequently, the recognition of the "right of nations to autonomy" is as absurd as that of the "right of nations to federation".

movements, an example which has lost none of its immense *practical* importance. It serves as a warning against that "servile haste" with which the philistines of all countries, colours and languages hurry to label as "utopian" the idea of altering the frontiers of states that were established by the violence and privileges of the landlords and bourgeoisie of one nation.

If the Irish and English proletariat had not accepted Marx's policy and had not made the secession of Ireland their slogan, this would have been the worst sort of opportunism, a neglect of their duties as democrats and socialists, and a concession to *English* reaction and the *English* bourgeoisie.

9. The 1903 Programme and Its Liquidators

The Minutes of the 1903 Congress, at which the Programme of the Russian Marxists was adopted, have become a great rarity, and the vast majority of the active members of the working-class movement today are unacquainted with the motives underlying the various points (the more so since not all the literature relating to it enjoys the blessings of legality...). It is therefore necessary to analyse the debate that took place at the 1903 Congress on the question under discussion.

Let us state first of all that however meagre the Russian Social-Democratic literature on the "right of nations to self-determination" may be, it nevertheless shows clearly that this right has always been understood to mean the right to secession. The Semkovskys, Liebmans and Yurkeviches who doubt this and declare that § 9 is "vague", etc., do so only because of their sheer ignorance or carelessness. As far back as 1902, Plekhanov, in *Zarya*, defended "the right to self-determination" in the draft programme, and wrote that this demand, while not obligatory upon bourgeois democrats, was "obligatory upon Social-Democrats". "If we were to forget it or hesitate to advance it," Plekhanov wrote, "for fear of offending the national prejudices of our fellow-countrymen of Great-Russian nationality, the call ... 'workers of all countries, unite!' would be a shameful lie on our lips...."[53]

This is a very apt description of the fundamental argument in favour of the point under consideration; so apt that it is not surprising that the "anythingarian" critics of our programme have been timidly avoiding it. The abandonment of this point, no matter for what motives, is *actually* a "shameful" concession to *Great-Russian* nationalism. But why Great-Russian, when it is a question of the right of *all* nations to self-determination? Because it refers to secession *from* the Great Russians. The interests of the *unity of the proletarians*, the interests of their class solidarity call for recognition of the right of *nations to secede*—that is what Plekhanov admitted twelve years ago in the words quoted above. Had our opportunists given thought to this they would probably not have talked so much nonsense about self-determination.

At the 1903 Congress, which adopted the draft programme that Plekhanov advocated, the main work was done by the *Programme Commission*. Unfortunately no Minutes of its proceedings were kept; they would have been particularly interesting on this point, for it was *only* in the Commission that the representatives of the Polish Social-Democrats, Warszawski and Hanecki, tried to defend their views and to dispute "recognition of the right to self-determination". Any reader who goes to the trouble of comparing their arguments (set forth in the speech by Warszawski and the statement by him and Hanecki, pp. 134-36 and 388-90 of the Congress Minutes) with those which Rosa Luxemburg advanced in her Polish article, which we have analysed, will find them identical.

How were these arguments treated by the Programme Commission of the Second Congress, where Plekhanov, more than anyone else, spoke against the Polish Marxists? They were mercilessly ridiculed! The absurdity of proposing to the Marxists of *Russia* that they should reject the recognition of the right of nations to self-determination was demonstrated so plainly and clearly that the Polish Marxists *did not even venture to repeat their arguments at the plenary meeting of the Congress!* They left the Congress, convinced of the hopelessness of their case at the supreme assembly of Marxists—Great-Russian, Jewish, Georgian, and Armenian.

Needless to say, this historic episode is of very great importance to everyone seriously interested in *his own* programme. The fact that the Polish Marxists' arguments were completely defeated at the Programme Commission of the Congress, and that the Polish Marxists gave up the attempt to defend their views at the plenary meeting of the Congress is very significant. No wonder Rosa Luxemburg maintained a "modest" silence about it in her article in 1908—the recollection of the Congress must have been too unpleasant! She also kept quiet about the ridiculously inept proposal made by Warszawski and Hanecki in 1903, on behalf of all Polish Marxists, to "amend" §9 of the Programme, a proposal which neither Rosa Luxemburg nor the other Polish Social-Democrats have ventured (or will ever venture) to repeat.

But although Rosa Luxemburg, concealing her defeat in 1903, has maintained silence over these facts, those who take an interest in the history of their Party will make it their business to ascertain them and give thought to their significance.

On leaving the 1903 Congress, Rosa Luxemburg's friends submitted the following statement:

"We propose that Clause 7 [now Clause 9] of the draft programme read as follows: §7. *Institutions guaranteeing full freedom of cultural development to all nations incorporated in the state.*" (P. 390 of the Minutes.)

Thus, the Polish Marxists at that time put forward views on the national question that were so vague that *instead of* self-determination they practically proposed the notorious "cultural-national autonomy", only under another name!

This sounds almost incredible, but unfortunately it is a fact. At the Congress itself, attended though it was by five Bundists with five votes and three Caucasians with six votes, without counting Kostrov's consultative voice, *not a single* vote was cast for the *rejection* of the clause about self-determination. Three votes were cast for the proposal to add "cultural-national autonomy" to this clause (in favour of Goldblatt's formula: "the establishment of institutions guaranteeing the nations full freedom of cultural development") and four votes for Lieber's formula ("the right of nations to freedom in their cultural development").

Now that a Russian liberal party—the Constitutional-Democratic Party—has appeared on the scene, we know that in *its* programme the political self-determination of nations has been replaced by "cultural self-determination". Rosa Luxemburg's Polish friends, therefore, were "*combating*" the nationalism of the P.S.P., and did it so successfully that they proposed the substitution of a *liberal* programme for the Marxist programme! And in the same breath they accused our programme of being opportunist; no wonder this accusation was received with laughter by the Programme Commission of the Second Congress!

How was "self-determination" understood by the delegates to the Second Congress, of whom, as we have seen, *not one* was opposed to "self-determination of nations"?

The following three extracts from the Minutes provide the answer:

"*Martynov* is of the opinion that the term 'self-determination' should not be given a broad interpretation; it merely means the right of a nation to establish itself as a separate polity, not regional self-government" (p. 171). Martynov was a member of the Programme Commission, in which the arguments of Rosa Luxemburg's friends were repudiated and ridiculed. Martynov was then an Economist in his views, and a violent opponent of *Iskra*; had he expressed an opinion that was not shared by the majority of the Programme Commission he would certainly have been repudiated.

Bundist Goldblatt was the first to speak when the Congress, after the Commission had finished its work, discussed § 8 (the present Clause 9) of the Programme. He said:

"No objections can be raised to the 'right to self-determination'. When a nation is fighting for independence, that should not be opposed. If Poland refuses to enter into lawful marriage with Russia, she should not be interfered with, as Plekhanov put it. I agree with this opinion within these limits" (pp. 175-76).

Plekhanov had not spoken on this subject at all at the plenary meeting of the Congress. Goldblatt was referring to what Plekhanov had said at the Programme Commission, where the "right to self-determination" had been explained in a simple yet detailed manner to mean the right to secession Lieber, who spoke after Goldblatt, remarked:

"Of course, if any nationality finds that it cannot live within the frontiers of Russia, the Party will not place any obstacles in its way" (p. 176).

The reader will see that at the Second Congress of the Party, which adopted the programme, it was unanimously understood that self-determination meant "only" the right to secession. Even the Bundists grasped this truth at the time, and it is only in our own deplorable times of continued counter-revolution and all sorts of "apostasy" that we can find people who, bold in their ignorance, declare that the programme is "vague". But before devoting time to these sorry would-be Social-Democrats, let us first finish with the attitude of the Poles to the programme.

They came to the Second Congress (1903) declaring that unity was necessary and imperative. But they left the Congress after their "reverses" in the Programme Commission, and their *last word* was a written statement, printed in the Minutes of the Congress, containing the above-mentioned proposal to *substitute* cultural-national autonomy for self-determination.

In 1906 the Polish Marxists joined the Party; *neither* upon joining *nor* afterwards (at the Congress of 1907, the conferences of 1907 and 1908, or the plenum of 1910) *did they introduce* a single proposal to amend § 9 of the Russian Programme!

That is a fact.

And, despite all utterances and assurances, this fact definitely proves that Rosa Luxemburg's friends regarded the question as having been settled by the debate at the Programme Commission of the Second Congress, as well as by the decision of that Congress, and that they tacitly acknowledged their mistake and corrected it by joining the Party in 1906, after they had left the Congress in 1903, without a single attempt to raise the question of amending § 9 of the Programme through *Party* channels.

Rosa Luxemburg's article appeared over her signature in 1908—of course, it never entered anyone's head to deny Party publicists the right to criticise the programme—and, *since* the writing of this article, *not a single* official body of the Polish Marxists has raised the question of revising §9.

Trotsky was therefore rendering a great disservice to certain admirers of Rosa Luxemburg when he wrote, on behalf of the editors of *Borba*,[54] in issue No. 2 of that publication (March 1914):

"The Polish Marxists consider that 'the right to national self-determination' is entirely devoid of political content and should be deleted from the programme" (p. 25).

The obliging Trotsky is more dangerous than an enemy! Trotsky could produce *no* proof, except "private conversations" (i.e., simply gossip, on which Trotsky always subsists), for classifying "Polish Marxists" in general as supporters of every article by Rosa Luxemburg. Trotsky presented the "Polish Marxists" as people devoid of honour and conscience, incapable of respecting even their own convictions and the programme of their Party. How obliging Trotsky is!

When, in 1903, the representatives of the Polish Marxists walked out of the Second Congress *over* the right to self-determination, Trotsky could have said *at the time* that they regarded this right as devoid of content and subject to deletion from the programme.

But after that the Polish Marxists *joined* the Party whose programme this was, and they have never introduced a motion to amend it.*

Why did Trotsky withhold these facts from the readers of his journal? Only because it pays him to speculate on fomenting differences between the Polish and the Russian opponents of liquidationism and to deceive the Russian workers on the question of the programme.

Trotsky has never yet held a firm opinion on any important question of Marxism. He always contrives to worm his way into the cracks of any given difference of opinion, and desert one side for the other. At the present moment he is in the company of the Bundists and the liquidators.

---

* We are informed that the Polish Marxists attended the Summer Conference of the Russian Marxists in 1913 with *only* a consultative voice and did not vote at all on the right to self-determination (secession), declaring their opposition to this right in general. Of course, they had a perfect right to act the way they did, and, as hitherto, to agitate in Poland against secession. But this is not quite what Trotsky said; for the Polish Marxists did not demand the "deletion" of § 9 "from the programme".

And these gentlemen do not stand on ceremony where the Party is concerned.

Listen to the Bundist Liebman.

"When, fifteen years ago," this gentleman writes, "the Russian Social-Democrats included the point about the right of every nationality to 'self-determination' in their programme, everyone [!] asked himself: What does this fashionable [!] term really mean? No answer was forthcoming [!]. This word was left [!] wrapped in mist. And indeed, at the time, it was difficult to dispel that mist. The moment had not come when this point could be made concrete—it was said—so let it remain wrapped in mist [!] for the time being and practice will show what content should be put into it."

Isn't it magnificent, the way this "ragamuffin" mocks at the Party programme?

And why does he mock at it?

Because he is an absolute ignoramus, who has never learnt anything or even read any Party history, but merely happened to land in liquidationist circles where going about in the nude is considered the "right" thing to do as far as knowledge of the Party and everything it stands for is concerned.

Pomyalovsky's seminary student boasts of having "spat into a barrel of sauerkraut".[55] The Bundist gentlemen have gone one better. They let the Liebmans loose to spit publicly into their own barrel. What do the Liebmans care about the fact that the International Congress has passed a decision, that at the Congress of their own Party two representatives of their own Bund proved that they were quite able (and what "severe" critics and determined enemies of *Iskra* they were!) to understand the meaning of "self-determination" and were even in agreement with it? And will it not be easier to liquidate the Party if the "Party publicists" (no jokes, please!) treat its history and programme after the fashion of the seminary student?

Here is a second "ragamuffin", Mr. Yurkevich of *Dzvin*. Mr. Yurkevich must have had the Minutes of the Second Congress before him, because he quotes Plekhanov, as repeated by Goldblatt, and shows that he is aware of the fact that self-determination can only mean the right to secession. This, however, does not prevent him from spreading slander about the Russian Marxists among the Ukrainian petty bourgeoisie, alleging that they stand for the "state integrity" of Russia. (No. 7-8, 1913, p. 83, etc.)

Of course, the Yurkeviches could not have invented a better method than such slander to alienate the Ukrainian democrats from the Great-Russian democrats. And such alienation is in line with the entire policy of the group of *Dzvin* publicists who advocate the *separation* of the Ukrainian workers *in a special* national organisation!*

It is quite appropriate, of course, that a group of nationalist philistines, who are engaged in splitting the ranks of the proletariat—and objectively this is the role of *Dzvin*—should disseminate such hopeless confusion on the national question. Needless to say, the Yurkeviches and Liebmans, who are "terribly" offended when they are called "near-Party men", do not say a word, not a single word, as to how *they* would like the problem of the right to secede to be settled in the programme.

But here is the third and principal "ragamuffin", Mr. Semkovsky, who, addressing a Great-Russian audience through the columns of a liquidationist newspaper, lashes at §9 of the Programme and at the same time declares that "for certain reasons he does not approve of the proposal" to delete this clause!

This is incredible, but it is a fact.

In August 1912, the liquidators' conference raised the national question officially. For eighteen months not a single article has appeared on the question of §9, except the one written by Mr. Semkovsky. And in this article the author *repudiates* the programme, "without approving", however, "for *certain* reasons" (is this a secrecy disease?) the proposal to amend it! We may be sure that it would be difficult to find anywhere in the world similar examples of opportunism, or even worse—renunciation of the Party, and a desire to liquidate it.

A single example will suffice to show what Semkovsky's arguments are like:

"What are we to do," he writes, "if the Polish proletariat wants to fight side by side with the proletariat of all Russia within the framework of a single state, while the reactionary classes of Polish society, on the contrary, want to separate Poland from Russia and obtain a majority of votes in favour of secession by referendum? Should we,

* See particularly Mr. Yurkevich's preface to Mr. Levinsky's book (written in Ukrainian) *Outline of the Development of the Ukrainian Working-Class Movement in Galicia*, Kiev, 1914.

Russian Social-Democrats in the central parliament, vote together with our Polish comrades *against* secession, or—in order not to violate the 'right to self-determination'—vote *for* secession?" (*Novaya Rabochaya Gazeta* No. 71.)

From this it is evident that Mr. Semkovsky does not even understand the *point at issue*! It did not occur to him that the right to secession presupposes the settlement of the question by a parliament (Diet, referendum, etc.) of the *seceding* region, *not* by a central parliament.

The childish perplexity over the question "What are we to do", if under democracy the majority are for reaction, serves to screen the real and live issue when *both* the Purishkeviches and the Kokoshkins consider the very idea of secession criminal! Perhaps the proletarians of *all* Russia ought not to fight the Purishkeviches and the Kokoshkins today, but should by-pass them and fight the reactionary classes of Poland!

Such is the sheer rubbish published in the liquidators' organ of which Mr. L. Martov is one of the ideological leaders, the selfsame L. Martov who drafted the programme and spoke in favour of its adoption in 1903, and even subsequently wrote in favour of the right to secede. Apparently L. Martov is now arguing according to the rule:

> *No clever man is needed there;*
> *Better send Read,*
> *And I shall wait and see.*[56]

He sends Read-Semkovsky along and allows our programme to be distorted and endlessly muddled up in a daily paper whose new readers are unacquainted with it!

Yes. Liquidationism has gone a long way—there are even very many prominent ex-Socialist-Democrats who have not a trace of Party spirit left in them.

Rosa Luxemburg cannot, of course, be classed with the Liebmans, Yurkeviches and Semkovskys, but the fact that it was this kind of people who seized upon her error shows with particular clarity the opportunism she has lapsed into.

10. Conclusion

To sum up.

As far as the theory of Marxism in general is concerned, the question of the right to self-determination presents no difficulty. No one can seriously question the London resolution of 1896, or the fact that self-determination implies only the right to secede, or that the formation of independent national states is the tendency in all bourgeois-democratic revolutions.

A difficulty is to some extent created by the fact that in Russia the proletariat of both the oppressed and oppressor nations are fighting, and must fight, side by side. The task is to preserve the unity of the proletariat's class struggle for socialism, and to resist all bourgeois and Black-Hundred nationalist influences. Where the oppressed nations are concerned, the separate organisation of the proletariat as an independent party sometimes leads to such a bitter struggle against local nationalism that the perspective becomes distorted and the nationalism of the oppressor nation is lost sight of.

But this distortion of perspective cannot last long. The experience of the joint struggle waged by the proletarians of various nations has demonstrated all too clearly that we must formulate political issues from the all-Russia, not the "Cracow" point of view. And in all-Russia politics it is the Purishkeviches and the Kokoshkins who are in the saddle. Their ideas predominate, and their persecution of non-Russians for "separatism", for *thinking* about secession, is being preached and practised in the Duma, in the schools, in the churches, in the barracks, and in hundreds and thousands of newspapers. It is this Great-Russian nationalist poison that is polluting the entire all-Russia political atmosphere. This is the misfortune of one nation, which, by subjugating other nations, is strengthening reaction throughout Russia. The memories of 1849 and 1863 form a living political tradition, which, unless great storms arise, threatens to hamper every democratic and *especially* every Social-Democratic movement for decades to come.

There can be no doubt that however natural the point of view of certain Marxists belonging to the oppressed nations (whose "misfortune" is sometimes that the masses of the population are blinded by the idea of their "own" national liberation) may appear at times, *in reality* the objective alignment of class forces in Russia makes refusal to advocate the right to self-determination tantamount to the worst opportunism, to the infection of the proletariat with the ideas of the Kokoshkins. And these ideas are, essentially, the ideas and the policy of the Purishkeviches.

Therefore, although Rosa Luxemburg's point of view could at first have been excused as being specifically Polish, "Cracow" narrow-mindedness,* it is inexcusable today, when nationalism and, above all, governmental Great-Russian nationalism, has everywhere gained ground, and when policy is being shaped by this *Great-Russian nationalism*. In actual fact, it is being seized upon by the opportunists of *all* nations, who fight shy of the idea of "storms" and "leaps", believe that the bourgeois-democratic revolution is over, and follow in the wake of the liberalism of the Kokoshkins.

Like any other nationalism, Great-Russian nationalism will pass through various phases, according to the classes that are dominant in the bourgeois country at any given time. Up to 1905, we almost exclusively knew national-reactionaries. After the revolution, *national-liberals* arose in our country.

In our country this is virtually the stand adopted both by the Octobrists and by the Cadets (Kokoshkin), i.e., by the whole of the present-day bourgeoisie.

Great-Russian national-democrats will *inevitably* appear later on. Mr. Peshekhonov, one of the founders of the "Popular Socialist" Party, already expressed this point of view (in the issue of *Russkoye Bogatstvo*[57] for August 1906) when he called for caution in regard to the peasants' nationalist prejudices. However much others may slander us Bolsheviks and accuse us of "idealising" the peasant, we always have made and always will make a clear distinction between peasant intelligence and peasant prejudice,

---

* It is not difficult to understand that the recognition by the Marxists of the *whole of Russia*, and first and foremost by the Great Russians, of the *right* of nations to secede in no way precludes *agitation* against secession by Marxists of a particular *oppressed* nation, just as the recognition of the right to divorce does not preclude agitation against divorce in a particular case. We think, therefore, that there will be an inevitable increase in the number of Polish Marxists who laugh at the non-existent "contradiction" now being "encouraged" by Semkovsky and Trotsky.

between peasant strivings for democracy and opposition to Purishkevich, and the peasant desire to make peace with the priest and the landlord.

Even now, and probably for a fairly long time to come, proletarian democracy must reckon with the nationalism of the Great-Russian peasants (not with the object of making concessions to it, but in order to combat it).* The awakening of nationalism among the oppressed nations, which became so pronounced after 1905 (let us recall, say, the group of "Federalist-Autonomists" in the First Duma, the growth of the Ukrainian movement, of the Moslem movement, etc.), will inevitably lead to greater nationalism among the Great-Russian petty bourgeoisie in town and countryside. The slower the democratisation of Russia, the more persistent, brutal and bitter will be the national persecution and bickering among the bourgeoisie of the various nations. The particularly reactionary nature of the Russian Purishkeviches will simultaneously give rise to (and strengthen) "separatist" tendencies among the various oppressed nationalities, which sometimes enjoy far greater freedom in neighbouring states.

In this situation, the proletariat of Russia is faced with a twofold or, rather, a two-sided task: to combat nationalism of every kind, above all, Great-Russian nationalism; to recognise, not only fully equal rights for all nations in general, but also equality of rights as regards polity, i.e., the right of nations to self-determination, to secession. And at the same time, it is their task, in the interests of a suc-

---

* It would be interesting to trace the changes that take place in Polish nationalism, for example, in the process of its transformation from gentry nationalism into bourgeois nationalism, and then into peasant nationalism. In his book *Das polnische Gemeinwesen im preussischen Staat* (*The Polish Community in the Prussian State*; there is a Russian translation), Ludwig Bernhard, who shares the view of a German Kokoshkin, describes a very typical phenomenon: the formation of a sort of "peasant republic" by the Poles in Germany in the form of a close alliance of the various co-operatives and other associations of *Polish* peasants in their struggle for nationality, religion, and "Polish" land. German oppression has welded the Poles together and segregated them, after first awakening the nationalism of the gentry, then of the bourgeoisie, and finally of the peasant masses (especially after the campaign the Germans launched in 1873 against the use of the Polish language in schools). Things are moving in the same direction in Russia, and not only with regard to Poland.

cessful struggle against all and every kind of nationalism among all nations, to preserve the unity of the proletarian struggle and the proletarian organisations, amalgamating these organisations into a close-knit international association, despite bourgeois strivings for national exclusiveness.

Complete equality of rights for all nations; the right of nations to self-determination; the unity of the workers of all nations—such is the national programme that Marxism, the experience of the whole world, and the experience of Russia, teach the workers.

———

This article had been set up when I received No. 3 of *Nasha Rabochaya Gazeta*, in which Mr. Vl. Kosovsky writes the following about the recognition of the right of all nations to self-determination:

"Taken mechanically from the resolution of the First Congress of the Party (1898), which in turn had borrowed it from the decisions of international socialist congresses, it was given, as is evident from the debate, the same meaning at the 1903 Congress as was ascribed to it by the Socialist International, i.e., political self-determination, the self-determination of nations in the field of political independence. Thus the formula: national self-determination, which implies the right to territorial separation, does not in any way affect the question of how national relations *within* a given state organism should be regulated for nationalities that cannot or have no desire to leave the existing state."

It is evident from this that Mr. Vl. Kosovsky has seen the Minutes of the Second Congress of 1903 and understands perfectly well the real (and only) meaning of the term self-determination. Compare this with the fact that the editors of the Bund newspaper *Zeit* let Mr. Liebman loose to scoff at the programme and to declare that it is vague! Queer "party" ethics among these Bundists.... The Lord alone knows why Kosovsky should declare that the Congress took over the principle of self-determination *mechanically*. Some people want to "object", but how, why, and for what reason—they do not know.

Written in February-May 1914

Published in April-June 1914
in the journal *Prosveshcheniye*
Nos. 4, 5 and 6
Signed: *V. Ilyin*

Collected Works, Vol. 20

ON THE NATIONAL PRIDE
OF THE GREAT RUSSIANS

What a lot of talk, argument and vociferation there is nowadays about nationality and the fatherland! Liberal and radical cabinet ministers in Britain, a host of "forward-looking" journalists in France (who have proved in full agreement with their reactionary colleagues), and a swarm of official Cadet and progressive scribblers in Russia (including several Narodniks and "Marxists")—all have effusive praise for the liberty and independence of their respective countries, the grandeur of the principle of national independence. Here one cannot tell where the venal eulogist of the butcher Nicholas Romanov or of the brutal oppressors of Negroes and Indians ends, and where the common philistine, who from sheer stupidity or spinelessness drifts with the stream, begins. Nor is that distinction important. We see before us an extensive and very deep ideological trend, whose origins are closely interwoven with the interests of the landowners and the capitalists of the dominant nations. Scores and hundreds of millions are being spent every year for the propaganda of ideas advantageous to those classes: it is a pretty big mill-race that takes its waters from all sources—from Menshikov, a chauvinist by conviction, to chauvinists for reason of opportunism or spinelessness, such as Plekhanov and Maslov, Rubanovich and Smirnov, Kropotkin and Burtsev.

Let us, Great-Russian Social-Democrats, also try to define our attitude to this ideological trend. It would be unseemly for us, representatives of a dominant nation in the far east of Europe and a goodly part of Asia, to forget the immense significance of the national question—especially in a country which has been rightly called the "prison of the peoples", and particularly at a time when, in the far east of Europe and in Asia, capitalism is awakening to life and self-consciousness a number of "new" nations, large and small; at a moment when the tsarist monarchy has called up millions of Great Russians and non-Russians, so as to "solve" a number of national problems in accordance with the interests of the Council of the United Nobility[58] and of the Guchkovs, Krestovnikovs, Dolgorukovs, Kutlers and Rodichevs.

Is a sense of national pride alien to us, Great-Russian class-conscious proletarians? Certainly not! We love our language and our country, and we are doing our very utmost to raise *her* toiling masses (i.e., nine-tenths of *her* population) to the level of a democratic and socialist consciousness. To us it is most painful to see and feel the outrages, the oppression and the humiliation our fair country suffers at the hands of the tsar's butchers, the nobles and the capitalists. We take pride in the resistance to these outrages put up from our midst, from the Great Russians; in *that* midst having produced Radishchev, the Decembrists and the revolutionary commoners of the seventies; in the Great-Russian working class having created, in 1905, a mighty revolutionary party of the masses; and in the Great-Russian peasantry having begun to turn towards democracy and set about overthrowing the clergy and the landed proprietors.

We remember that Chernyshevsky, the Great-Russian democrat, who dedicated his life to the cause of revolution, said half a century ago: "A wretched nation, a nation of slaves, from top to bottom—all slaves."[59] The overt and covert Great-Russian slaves (slaves with regard to the tsarist monarchy) do not like to recall these words. Yet, in our opinion, these were words of genuine love for our country, a love distressed by the absence of a revolutionary spirit in the masses of the Great-Russian people. There was none of that spirit at the time. There is little of it now, but it already exists. We are full of national pride because the Great-Russian nation, *too*, has created a revolutionary class, because it, *too*, has proved capable of providing mankind with great models of the struggle for freedom and socialism, and not only with great pogroms, rows of gallows, dungeons, great famines and great servility to priests, tsars, landowners and capitalists.

We are full of a sense of national pride, and for that very reason we *particularly* hate *our* slavish past (when the landed nobility led the peasants into war to stifle the freedom of Hungary, Poland, Persia and China), and our slavish present, when these selfsame landed proprietors, aided by the capitalists, are leading us into a war in order to throttle Poland and the Ukraine, crush the democratic movement in Persia and China, and strengthen the gang of Romanovs, Bobrinskys and Purishkeviches, who are a disgrace to our Great-Russian national dignity. Nobody is to be blamed for being born a slave; but a slave who not only eschews a striving for freedom but justifies and eulogises his slavery (e.g., calls the throttling of Poland and the Ukraine, etc., a "defence of the fatherland" of the Great Russians)—such a slave is a lickspittle and a boor, who arouses a legitimate feeling of indignation, contempt, and loathing.

"No nation can be free if it oppresses other nations,"[60] said Marx and Engels, the greatest representatives of consistent nineteenth century democracy, who became the teachers of the revolutionary proletariat. And, full of a sense of national pride, we Great-Russian workers want, come what may, a free and independent, a democratic, republican and proud Great Russia, one that will base its relations with its neighbours on the human principle of equality, and not on the feudalist principle of privilege, which is so degrading to a great nation. Just because we want that, we say: it is impossible, in the twentieth century and in Europe (even in the far east of Europe), to "defend the fatherland" otherwise than by using every revolutionary means to combat the monarchy, the landowners and the capitalists of one's *own* fatherland, i.e., the *worst* enemies of our country. We say that the Great Russians cannot "defend the fatherland" otherwise than by desiring the defeat of tsarism in any war, this as the lesser evil to nine-tenths of the inhabitants of Great Russia. For tsarism not only oppresses those nine-tenths economically and politically, but also demoralises, degrades, dishonours and prostitutes them by teaching them to oppress other nations and to cover up this shame with hypocritical and quasi-patriotic phrases.

The objection may be advanced that, besides tsarism and under its wing, another historical force has arisen and become strong, viz., Great-Russian capitalism, which is carrying on progressive work by economically centralising and welding together vast regions. This objection, however, does not excuse, but on the contrary still more condemns our socialist-chauvinists, who should be called tsarist-Purishkevich socialists (just as Marx called the Lassalleans Royal-Prussian socialists). Let us even assume that history will decide in favour of Great-Russian dominant-nation capitalism, and against the hundred and one small nations. That is not impossible, for the entire history of capital is one of violence and plunder, blood and corruption. We do not advocate preserving small nations at all costs; *other conditions being equal*, we are decidedly for centralisation and are opposed to the petty-bourgeois ideal of federal relationships. Even if our assumption were true, however, it is, firstly, not our business, or that of democrats (let alone of socialists), to help Romanov-Bobrinsky-Purishkevich throttle the Ukraine, etc. In his own Junker fashion, Bismarck accomplished a progressive historical task, but he would be a fine "Marxist" indeed who, on such grounds, thought of justifying socialist support for Bismarck! Moreover, Bismarck promoted economic development by bringing together the disunited Germans, who were being oppressed by other nations. The economic prosperity and rapid development of Great Russia, however, require that the country be liberated from Great-Russian oppression of other nations—that is the difference that our admirers of the true-Russian would-be Bismarcks overlook.

Secondly, if history were to decide in favour of Great-Russian dominant-nation capitalism, it follows hence that the *socialist* role of the Great-Russian proletariat, as the principal driving force of the communist revolution engendered by capitalism, will be all the greater. The proletarian revolution calls for a prolonged education of the workers in the spirit of the *fullest* national equality and brotherhood. Consequently, the interests of the Great-Russian proletariat require that the masses be systematically educated to champion—most resolutely, consistently, boldly and in a revolutionary manner—complete equality and the right to self-determination for all the nations oppressed by the Great Russians. The interests of the Great Russians' national pride (understood not in the slavish sense) coincide with the *socialist* interests of the Great-Russian (and all other) proletarians. Our model will always be Marx, who, after living in Britain for decades and becoming half-English, demanded freedom and national independence for Ireland in the interests of the socialist movement of the British workers.

In the second hypothetical case we have considered, our home-grown socialist-chauvinists, Plekhanov, etc., etc., will prove traitors, not only to their own country—a free and democratic Great Russia, but also to the proletarian brotherhood of all the nations of Russia, i.e., to the cause of socialism.

Sotsial-Demokrat No. 35, December 12, 1914

Collected Works, Vol. 21

THE SOCIALIST REVOLUTION AND THE RIGHT OF NATIONS TO SELF-DETERMINATION

THESES

1. Imperialism, Socialism and the Liberation of Oppressed Nations

Imperialism is the highest stage in the development of capitalism. In the foremost countries capital has outgrown the bounds of national states, has replaced competition by monopoly and has created all the objective conditions for the achievement of socialism. In Western Europe and in the United States, therefore, the revolutionary struggle of the proletariat for the overthrow of capitalist governments and the expropriation of the bourgeoisie is on the order of the day. Imperialism forces the masses into this struggle by sharpening class contradictions on a tremendous scale, by worsening the conditions of the masses both economically—trusts, high cost of living—and politically—the growth of militarism, more frequent wars, more powerful reaction, the intensification and expansion of national oppression and colonial plunder. Victorious socialism must necessarily establish a full democracy and, consequently, not only introduce full equality of nations but also realise the right of the oppressed nations to self-determination, i.e., the right to free political separation. Socialist parties which did not show by all their activity, both now, during the revolution, and after its victory, that they would liberate the enslaved nations and build up relations with them on the basis of a free union—and free union is a false phrase without the right to secede—these parties would be betraying socialism.

Democracy, of course, is also a form of state which must disappear when the state disappears, but that will only take place in the transition from conclusively victorious and consolidated socialism to full communism.

2. The Socialist Revolution and the Struggle for Democracy

The socialist revolution is not a single act, it is not one battle on one front, but a whole epoch of acute class conflicts, a long series of battles on all fronts, i.e., on all questions of economics and politics, battles that can only end in the expropriation of the bourgeoisie. It would be a radical mistake to think that the struggle for democracy was capable of diverting the proletariat from the socialist revolution or of hiding, overshadowing it, etc. On the contrary, in the same way as there can be no victorious socialism that does not practise full democracy, so the proletariat cannot prepare for its victory over the bourgeoisie without an all-round, consistent and revolutionary struggle for democracy.

It would be no less a mistake to remove one of the points of the democratic programme, for example, the point on the self-determination of nations, on the grounds of it being "impracticable" or "illusory" under imperialism. The contention that the right of nations to self-determination is impracticable within the bounds of capitalism can be understood either in the absolute, economic sense, or in the conditional, political sense.

In the first case it is radically incorrect from the standpoint of theory. First, in that sense, such things as, for example, labour money, or the abolition of crises, etc., are impracticable under capitalism. It is absolutely untrue that the self-determination of nations is *equally* impracticable. Secondly, even the one example of the secession of Norway from Sweden in 1905 is sufficient to refute "impracticability" in that sense. Thirdly, it would be absurd to deny that some slight change in the political and strategic relations of, say, Germany and Britain, might today or tomorrow make the formation of a new Polish, Indian and other similar state fully "practicable". Fourthly, finance capital, in its drive to expand, can "freely" buy or bribe the freest democratic or republican government and the elective officials of any, even an "independent", country. The domination of finance capital and of capital in general is not to be abolished by *any* reforms in the sphere of political democracy; and self-determination belongs wholly and exclusively to this sphere. This domination of finance capital, however, does not in the least nullify the significance of political democracy as a freer, wider and clearer *form* of class oppression and class struggle. Therefore all arguments about the "impracticability", in the economic sense, of one of the demands of political democracy under capitalism are reduced to a theoretically incorrect definition of the general and basic relationships of capitalism and of political democracy as a whole.

In the second case the assertion is incomplete and inaccurate. This is because not only the right of nations to self-determination, but *all* the fundamental demands of political democracy are only partially "practicable" under imperialism, and then in a distorted form and by way of exception (for example, the secession of Norway from Sweden in 1905). The demand for the immediate liberation of the colonies that is put forward by all revolutionary Social-Democrats is also "impracticable" under capitalism without a series of revolutions. But from this it does not by any means follow that Social-Democracy should reject the immediate and most determined struggle for *all* these demands—such a rejection would only play into the hands of the bourgeoisie and reaction—but, on the contrary, it follows that these demands must be formulated and put through in a revolutionary and not a reformist manner, going beyond the bounds of bourgeois legality, breaking them down, going beyond speeches in parliament and verbal protests, and drawing the masses into decisive action, extending and intensifying the struggle for every fundamental democratic demand up to a direct proletarian onslaught on the bourgeoisie, i.e., up to the socialist revolution that expropriates the bourgeoisie. The socialist revolution may flare up not only through some big strike, street demonstration or hunger riot or a military insurrection or colonial revolt, but also as a result of a political crisis such as the Dreyfus case[61] or the Zabern incident,[62] or in connection with a referendum on the secession of an oppressed nation, etc.

Increased national oppression under imperialism does not mean that Social-Democracy should reject what the bourgeoisie call the "utopian" struggle for the freedom of nations to secede but, on the contrary, it should make greater use of the conflicts that arise in this sphere, *too*, as grounds for mass action and for revolutionary attacks on the bourgeoisie.

3. The Significance of the Right to Self-Determination and Its Relation to Federation

The right of nations to self-determination implies exclusively the right to independence in the political sense, the right to free political separation from the oppressor nation. Specifically, this demand for political democracy implies complete freedom to agitate for secession and for a referendum on secession by the seceding nation. This demand, therefore, is not the equivalent of a demand for separation, fragmentation and the formation of small states. It implies only a consistent expression of struggle against all national oppression. The closer a democratic state system is to complete freedom to secede the less frequent and less ardent will the desire for separation be in practice, because big states afford indisputable advantages, both from the standpoint of economic progress and from that of the interests of the masses and, furthermore, these advantages increase with the growth of capitalism. Recognition of self-determination is not synonymous with recognition of federation as a principle. One may be a determined opponent of that principle and a champion of democratic centralism but still prefer federation to national inequality as the only way to full democratic centralism. It was from this standpoint that Marx, who was a centralist, preferred even the federation of Ireland and England to the forcible subordination of Ireland to the English.[63]

The aim of socialism is not only to end the division of mankind into tiny states and the isolation of nations in any form, it is not only to bring the nations closer together but to integrate them. And it is precisely in order to achieve this aim that we must, on the one hand, explain to the masses the reactionary nature of Renner's and Otto Bauer's idea of so-called "cultural and national autonomy"[64] and, on the other, demand the liberation of oppressed nations in a clearly and precisely formulated political programme that takes special account of the hypocrisy and cowardice of socialists in the oppressor nations, and not in general nebulous phrases, not in empty declamations and not by way of "relegating" the question until socialism has been achieved. In the same way as mankind can arrive at the abolition of classes only through a transition period of the dictatorship of the oppressed class, it can arrive at the inevitable integration of nations only through a transition period of the complete emancipation of all oppressed nations, i.e., their freedom to secede.

4. The Proletarian-Revolutionary Presentation of the Question of the Self-Determination of Nations

The petty bourgeoisie had put forward not only the demand for the self-determination of nations but *all* the points of our democratic minimum programme long *before*, as far back as the seventeenth and eighteenth centuries. They are still putting them *all* forward in a utopian manner because they fail to see the class struggle and its increased intensity under democracy, and because they believe in "peaceful" capitalism. That is the exact nature of the utopia of a peaceful union of equal nations under imperialism which deceives the people and which is defended by Kautsky's followers. The programme of Social-Democracy, as a counter-balance to this petty-bourgeois, opportunist utopia, must postulate the division of nations into oppressor and oppressed as basic, significant and inevitable under imperialism.

The proletariat of the oppressor nations must not confine themselves to general, stereotyped phrases against annexation and in favour of the equality of nations in general, such as any pacifist bourgeois will repeat. The proletariat cannot remain silent on the question of the *frontiers* of a state founded on national oppression, a question so "unpleasant" for the imperialist bourgeoisie. The proletariat must struggle against the enforced retention of oppressed nations within the bounds of the given state, which means that they must fight for the right to self-determination. The proletariat must demand freedom of political separation for the colonies and nations oppressed by "their own" nation. Otherwise, the internationalism of the proletariat would be nothing but empty words; neither confidence nor class solidarity would be possible between the workers of the oppressed and the oppressor nations; the hypocrisy of the reformists and Kautskyites, who defend self-determination but remain silent about the nations oppressed by "their own" nation and kept in "their own" state by force, would remain unexposed.

On the other hand, the socialists of the oppressed nations must, in particular, defend and implement the full and unconditional unity, including organisational unity, of the workers of the oppressed nation and those of the oppressor nation. Without this it is impossible to defend the independent policy of the proletariat and their class solidarity with the proletariat of other countries in face of all manner of intrigues, treachery and trickery on the part of the bourgeoisie. The bourgeoisie of the oppressed nations persistently utilise the slogans of national liberation to deceive the workers; in their internal policy they use these slogans for reactionary agreements with the bourgeoisie of the dominant nation (for example, the Poles in Austria and Russia who come to terms with reactionaries for the oppression of the Jews and Ukrainians); in their foreign policy they strive to come to terms with one of the rival imperialist powers for the sake of implementing their predatory plans (the policy of the small Balkan states, etc.).

The fact that the struggle for national liberation against one imperialist power may, under certain conditions, be utilised by another "great" power for its own, equally imperialist, aims, is just as unlikely to make the Social-Democrats refuse to recognise the right of nations to self-determination as the numerous cases of bourgeois utilisation of republican slogans for the purpose of political deception and financial plunder (as in the Romance countries, for example) are unlikely to make the Social-Democrats reject their republicanism.*

5. Marxism and Proudhonism
on the National Question

In contrast to the petty-bourgeois democrats, Marx regarded every democratic demand without exception not as an absolute, but as an historical expression of the struggle of the masses of the people, led by the bourgeoisie, against feudalism. There is not one of these demands which could not serve and has not served, under certain circumstances, as an instrument in the hands of the bourgeoisie for deceiving the workers. To single out, in this respect, one of the demands of political democracy, specifically, the self-determination of nations, and to oppose it to the rest, is fundamentally wrong in theory. In practice, the proletariat can retain its independence only by subordinating its struggle for all democratic demands, not excluding the demand for a republic, to its revolutionary struggle for the overthrow of the bourgeoisie.

On the other hand, in contrast to the Proudhonists who "denied" the national problem "in the name of social revolution", Marx, mindful in the first place of the interests of the proletarian class struggle in the advanced countries, put the fundamental principle of internationalism and socialism in the foreground—namely, that no nation can be free if it oppresses other nations. It was from the stand-

---

* It would, needless to say, be quite ridiculous to reject the right to self-determination on the grounds that it implies "defence of the fatherland". With equal right, i.e., with equal lack of seriousness, the social-chauvinists of 1914-16 refer to any of the demands of democracy (to its republicanism, for example) and to any formulation of the struggle against national oppression in order to justify "defence of the fatherland". Marxism deduces the defence of the fatherland in wars, for example, in the great French Revolution or the wars of Garibaldi, in Europe, and the renunciation of defence of the fatherland in the imperialist war of 1914-16, from an analysis of the concrete historical peculiarities of each individual war and never from any "general principle", or any one point of a programme.

point of the interests of the German workers' revolutionary movement that Marx in 1848 demanded that victorious democracy in Germany should proclaim and grant freedom to the nations oppressed by the Germans. It was from the standpoint of the revolutionary struggle of the English workers that Marx, in 1869, demanded the separation of Ireland from England, and added: "...even if federation should follow upon separation."[65] Only by putting forward this demand was Marx really educating the English workers in the spirit of internationalism. Only in this way could he counterpose the opportunists and bourgeois reformism —which even to this day, half a century later, has not carried out the Irish "reform"—with a revolutionary solution of the given historical task. Only in this way could Marx maintain—unlike the apologists of capital who shout that the freedom of small nations to secede is utopian and impracticable and that not only economic but also political concentration is progressive—that this concentration is progressive when it is *non*-imperialist, and that nations should not be brought together by force, but by a free union of the proletarians of all countries. Only in this way could Marx, in opposition to the merely verbal, and often hypocritical, recognition of the equality and self-determination of nations, advocate the revolutionary action of the masses in the settlement of national questions *as well*. The imperialist war of 1914-16, and the Augean stables of hypocrisy on the part of the opportunists and Kautskyites that it has exposed, have strikingly confirmed the correctness of Marx's policy, which should serve as a model for all advanced countries, for all of them are now oppressing other nations.*

* Reference is often made—e.g., recently by the German chauvinist Lensch in *Die Glocke*[66] Nos. 8 and 9—to the fact that Marx's objection to the national movement of certain peoples, to that of the Czechs in 1848, for example, refutes the necessity of recognising the self-determination of nations from the Marxist standpoint. But this is incorrect, for in 1848 there were historical and political grounds for drawing a distinction between "reactionary" and revolutionary-democratic nations. Marx was right to condemn the former and defend the latter.[67] The right to self-determination is one of the demands of democracy which must naturally be subordinated to its general interests. In 1848 and the following years these general interests consisted primarily in combating tsarism.

6. Three Types of Countries with Respect to the Self-Determination of Nations

In this respect, countries must be divided into three main types.

First, the advanced capitalist countries of Western Europe and the United States. In these countries progressive bourgeois national movements came to an end long ago. Every one of these "great" nations oppresses other nations both in the colonies and at home. The tasks of the proletariat of these ruling nations are the same as those of the proletariat in England in the nineteenth century in relation to Ireland.*

Secondly, Eastern Europe: Austria, the Balkans and particularly Russia. Here it was the twentieth century that particularly developed the bourgeois-democratic national movements and intensified the national struggle. The tasks of the proletariat in these countries, both in completing their bourgeois-democratic reforms, and rendering assistance to the socialist revolution in other countries, cannot be carried out without championing the right of nations to self-determination. The most difficult and most important task in this is to unite the class struggle of the workers of the oppressor nations with that of the workers of the oppressed nations.

Thirdly, the semi-colonial countries, such as China, Persia and Turkey, and all the colonies, which have a combined population of 1,000 million. In these countries the

---

* In some small states which have kept out of the war of 1914-16—Holland and Switzerland, for example—the bourgeoisie makes extensive use of the "self-determination of nations" slogan to justify participation in the imperialist war. This is a motive inducing the Social-Democrats in such countries to repudiate self-determination. Wrong arguments are being used to defend a correct proletarian policy, the repudiation of "defence of the fatherland" in an *imperialist* war. This results in a distortion of Marxism in theory, and in practice leads to a peculiar small-nation narrow-mindedness, neglect of the *hundreds of millions* of people in nations that are enslaved by the "dominant" nations. Comrade Gorter, in his excellent pamphlet *Imperialism, War and Social-Democracy*, wrongly rejects the principle of self-determination of nations, but correctly *applies* it, when he demands the *immediate* granting of "political and *national* independence" to the Dutch Indies and exposes the Dutch opportunists who refuse to put forward this demand and to fight for it.

bourgeois-democratic movements either have hardly begun, or have still a long way to go. Socialists must not only demand the unconditional and immediate liberation of the colonies without compensation—and this demand in its political expression signifies nothing else than the recognition of the right to self-determination; they must also render determined support to the more revolutionary elements in the bourgeois-democratic movements for national liberation in these countries and assist their uprising—or revolutionary war, in the event of one—*against* the imperialist powers that oppress them.

7. Social-Chauvinism and the Self-Determination of Nations

The imperialist epoch and the war of 1914-16 has laid special emphasis on the struggle against chauvinism and nationalism in the leading countries. There are two main trends on the self-determination of nations among the social-chauvinists, that is, among the opportunists and Kautskyites, who hide the imperialist, reactionary nature of the war by applying to it the "defence of the father-land" concept.

On the one hand, we see quite undisguised servants of the bourgeoisie who defend annexation on the plea that imperialism and political concentration are progressive, and who deny what they call the utopian, illusory, petty-bourgeois, etc., right to self-determination. This includes Cunow, Parvus and the extreme opportunists in Germany, some of the Fabians and trade union leaders in England, and the opportunists in Russia: Semkovsky, Liebman, Yurkevich, etc.

On the other hand, we see the Kautskyites, among whom are Vandervelde, Renaudel, many pacifists in Britain and France, and others. They favour unity with the former and in practice are completely identified with them; they defend the right to self-determination hypocritically and by words alone: they consider "excessive" ("*zu viel verlangt*": Kautsky in *Die Neue Zeit*, May 21, 1915) the demand for free political separation, they do not defend the necessity for revolutionary tactics on the part of the socialists of the oppressor nations in particular but, on the contrary, obscure their revolutionary obligations, justify their opportunism, make easy for them their deception of the people, and avoid the very question of the *frontiers* of a state forcefully retaining underprivileged nations within its bounds, etc.

Both are equally opportunist, they prostitute Marxism, having lost all ability to understand the theoretical sig-nificance and practical urgency of the tactics which Marx explained with Ireland as an example.

As for annexations, the question has become particularly urgent in connection with the war. But what is annexation? It is quite easy to see that a protest against annexations either boils down to recognition of the self-determination of nations or is based on the pacifist phrase that defends the *status quo* and is hostile to *any*, even revolutionary, violence. Such a phrase is fundamentally false and incom-patible with Marxism.

8. The Concrete Tasks of the Proletariat in the Immediate Future

The socialist revolution may begin in the very near future. In this case the proletariat will be faced with the immediate task of winning power, expropriating the banks and effecting other dictatorial measures. The bourgeoisie— and especially the intellectuals of the Fabian and Kaut-skyite type—will, at such a moment, strive to split and check the revolution by foisting limited, democratic aims on it. Whereas *any* purely democratic demands are in a certain sense liable to act as a hindrance to the revolution, provided the proletarian attack on the pillars of bour-geois power has begun, the necessity to proclaim and grant liberty to *all* oppressed peoples (i.e., their right to self-determination) will be as urgent in the socialist revolution as it was for the victory of the bourgeois-democratic rev-olution in, say, Germany in 1848, or Russia in 1905.

It is possible, however, that five, ten or more years will elapse before the socialist revolution begins. This will be the time for the revolutionary education of the masses in a spirit that will make it impossible for socialist-chauvinists and opportunists to belong to the working-class party and gain a victory, as was the case in 1914-16. The socialists must explain to the masses that British socialists who do not demand freedom to separate for the colonies and Ireland, German socialists who do not demand freedom to separate for the colonies, the Alsatians, Danes and Poles, and who do not extend their revolutionary propaganda and revolutionary mass activity directly to the sphere of struggle against national oppression, or who do not make use of such incidents as that at Zabern for the broadest illegal propaganda among the proletariat of the oppressor nation, for street demonstrations and revolutionary mass action, Russian socialists who do not demand freedom to separate for Finland, Poland, the Ukraine, etc., etc.—that such socialists act as chauvinists and lackeys of bloodstained and filthy imperialist monarchies and the imperialist bourgeoisie.

9. The Attitude of Russian and Polish Social-Democrats and of the Second International to Self-Determination

The differences between the revolutionary Social-Democrats of Russia and the Polish Social-Democrats on the question of self-determination came out into the open as early as 1903, at the Congress which adopted the Programme of the R.S.D.L. Party, and which, despite the protest by the Polish Social-Democrat delegation, inserted Clause 9, recognising the right of nations to self-determination. Since then the Polish Social-Democrats have on no occasion repeated, in the name of their party, the proposal to remove Clause 9 from our Party's Programme, or to replace it by some other formula.

In Russia, where the oppressed nations account for no less than 57 per cent of the population, or over 100 million, where they occupy mostly the border regions, where some of them are more highly cultured than the Great Russians, where the political system is especially barbarous and medieval, where the bourgeois-democratic revolution has not been consummated—there, in Russia, recognition of the right of nations oppressed by tsarism to free secession from Russia is absolutely obligatory for Social-Democrats, for the furtherance of their democratic and socialist aims. Our Party, re-established in January 1912, adopted a resolution in 1913[68] reaffirming the right to self-determination and explaining it in precisely the above concrete sense. The rampage of Great-Russian chauvinism in 1914-16 both among the bourgeoisie and among the opportunist socialists (Rubanovich, Plekhanov, *Nashe Dyelo*,[69] etc.) has given us even more reason to insist on this demand and to regard those who deny it as actual supporters of Great-Russian chauvinism and tsarism. Our Party declares that it most emphatically declines to accept any responsibility for such actions against the right to self-determination.

The latest formulation of the position of the Polish Social-Democrats on the national question (the declaration of the Polish Social-Democrats at the Zimmerwald Conference[70]) contains the following ideas:

The declaration condemns the German and other governments that regard the "Polish regions" as a pawn in the forthcoming compensation game, "*depriving the Polish people of the opportunity of deciding their own fate themselves*". "Polish Social-Democrats resolutely and solemnly protest against the *carving up and parcelling out of a whole country*".... They flay the socialists who left it to the Hohenzollerns "*to liberate the oppressed peoples*". They express the conviction that only participation in the approaching struggle of the international revolutionary proletariat, the struggle for socialism, "*will break the fetters of national oppression* and destroy *all forms of foreign* rule, will ensure for *the Polish people* the possibility of free all-round development as an *equal* member of a concord of nations". The declaration recognises that "*for the Poles*" the war is "*doubly* fratricidal". (*Bulletin of the International Socialist Committee* No. 2, September 27, 1915, p. 15. Russian translation in the symposium *The International and the War*, p. 97.)

These propositions do not differ in substance from recognition of the right of nations to self-determination, although their political formulations are even vaguer and more indeterminate than those of most programmes and resolutions of the Second International. Any attempt to express these ideas as precise political formulations and to define their applicability to the capitalist system or only to the socialist system will show even more clearly the mistake the Polish Social-Democrats make in denying the self-determination of nations.

The decision of the London International Socialist Congress of 1896, which recognised the self-determination of nations, should be supplemented on the basis of the above theses by specifying: (1) the particular urgency of this demand under imperialism, (2) the political conventionalism and class content of all the demands of political democracy, the one under discussion included, (3) the necessity to distinguish the concrete tasks of the Social-Democrats of the oppressor nations from those of the Social-Democrats of the oppressed nations, (4) the inconsistent, purely verbal recognition of self-determination by the opportunists and the Kautskyites, which is, therefore, hypocritical in its political significance, (5) the actual identity of the chauvinists and those Social-Democrats, especially those of the Great Powers (Great Russians, Anglo-Americans, Germans, French, Italians, Japanese, etc.), who do not uphold the freedom to secede for colonies and nations oppressed by "their own" nations, (6) the necessity to subordinate the struggle for the demand under discussion and for all the basic demands of political democracy directly to the revolutionary mass struggle for the overthrow of the bourgeois governments and for the achievement of socialism.

The introduction into the International of the viewpoint of certain small nations, especially that of the Polish Social-Democrats, who have been led by their struggle against the Polish bourgeoisie, which deceives the people with its nationalist slogans, to the incorrect denial of self-determination, would be a theoretical mistake, a substitution of Proudhonism for Marxism implying in practice involuntary support for the most dangerous chauvinism and opportunism of the Great-Power nations.

Editorial Board of "Sotsial-Demokrat",
Central Organ of R.S.D.L.P.

Postscript. In *Die Neue Zeit* for March 3, 1916, which has just appeared, Kautsky openly holds out the hand of

Christian reconciliation to Austerlitz, a representative of the foulest German chauvinism, rejecting freedom of separation for the oppressed nations of Hapsburg Austria but recognising it for *Russian* Poland, as a menial service to Hindenburg and Wilhelm II. One could not have wished for a better self-exposure of Kautskyism!

Written January-February 1916

Printed in April 1916
in the magazine *Vorbote* No. 2
Printed in Russian in October 1916
in *Sbornik Sotsial-Demokrata* No. 1

Collected Works, Vol. 22

THE DISCUSSION ON SELF-DETERMINATION SUMMED UP

Issue No. 2 of the *Herald* (*Vorbote*[71] No. 2, April 1916), the Marxist journal of the Zimmerwald Left, published theses for and against the self-determination of nations, signed by the Editorial Board of our Central Organ, *Sotsial-Demokrat*, and by the Editorial Board of the organ of the Polish Social-Democratic opposition, *Gazeta Robotnicza*. Above the reader will find a reprint of the former* and a translation of the latter theses.[72] This is practically the first time that the question has been presented so extensively in the international field: it was raised only in respect of Poland in the discussion carried on in the German Marxist journal *Neue Zeit* twenty years ago, 1895-96, before the London International Socialist Congress of 1896, by Rosa Luxemburg, Karl Kautsky and the Polish "independents" (champions of the independence of Poland, the Polish Socialist Party), who represented three different views.[73] Since then, as far as we know, the question of self-determination has been discussed at all systematically only by the Dutch and the Poles. Let us hope that the *Herald* will succeed in promoting the discussion of this question, so urgent today, among the British, Americans, French, Germans and Italians. Official socialism, represented both by direct supporters of "their own" governments, the Plekhanovs, Davids and Co., and their undercover defenders of opportunism, the Kautskyites (among them Axelrod, Martov, Chkheidze and others), has told so many lies on this question that for a long time there

---

* See this pamphlet, pp. 110-24.—*Ed.*

will inevitably be efforts, on the one hand, to maintain silence and evade the issue, and, on the other, workers' demands for "direct answers" to these "accursed questions". We shall try to keep our readers informed of the struggle between the trends among socialists abroad.

This question is of specific importance to us Russian Social-Democrats; the present discussion is a continuation of the one that took place in 1903 and 1913[74]; during the war this question has been the cause of some wavering in the thinking of Party members; it has been made more acute by the trickery of such prominent leaders of the Gvozdyov or chauvinist workers' party as Martov and Chkheidze, in their efforts to evade the substance of the problem. It is essential, therefore, to sum up at least the initial results of the discussion that has been started in the international field.

It will be seen from the theses that our Polish comrades provide us with a direct answer to some of our arguments, for example, on Marxism and Proudhonism. In most cases, however, they do not answer us directly, but indirectly, by opposing *their* assertions to ours. Let us examine both their direct and indirect answers.

1. Socialism and the Self-Determination of Nations

We have affirmed that it would be a betrayal of socialism to refuse to implement the self-determination of nations under socialism. We are told in reply that "the right of self-determination is not applicable to a socialist society". The difference is a radical one. Where does it stem from?

"We know," runs our opponents' reasoning, "that socialism will abolish every kind of national oppression since it abolishes the class interests that lead to it...." What has this argument about the *economic* prerequisites for the abolition of national oppression, which are very well known and undisputed, to do with a discussion of *one* of the forms of *political* oppression, namely, the forcible retention of one nation within the state frontiers of another? This is nothing but an attempt to evade political questions! And subsequent arguments further convince us that our judgement is right:

"We have no reason to believe that in a socialist society, the nation will exist as an economic and political unit. It will in all probability assume the character of a cultural and linguistic unit only, because the territorial division of a socialist cultural zone, if practised at all, can be made only according to the needs of production and, furthermore, the question of such a division will naturally not be decided by individual nations alone and in possession of full sovereignty (as is required by 'the right to self-determination'), but will be *determined jointly* by all the citizens concerned...."

Our Polish comrades like this last argument, on *joint* determination instead of *self*-determination, so much that they repeat it *three times* in their theses! Frequency of repetition, however, does not turn this Octobrist and reactionary argument into a Social-Democratic argument. All reactionaries and bourgeois grant to nations forcibly retained within the frontiers of a given state the right to "determine jointly" their fate in a common parliament. Wilhelm II also gives the Belgians the right to "determine jointly" the fate of the German Empire in a common German parliament.

Our opponents try to evade precisely the point at issue, the only one that is up for discussion—the right to secede. This would be funny if it were not so tragic!

Our very first thesis said that the liberation of oppressed nations implies a dual transformation in the political sphere: (1) the full equality of nations. This is not disputed and applies only to what takes place within the state; (2) freedom of political separation.* This refers to the demarcation of state frontiers. This *only* is disputed. But it is precisely this that our opponents remain silent about. They do not want to think either about state frontiers or even about the state as such. This is a sort of "imperialist Economism" like the old Economism of 1894-1902, which argued in this way: capitalism is victorious, *therefore* political questions are a waste of time. Imperialism is victorious, *therefore* political questions are a waste of time! Such an apolitical theory is extremely harmful to Marxism.

In his *Critique of the Gotha Programme*, Marx wrote: "Between capitalist and communist society lies the period

_____
* See this pamphlet, p. 110.—*Ed.*

of the revolutionary transformation of the one into the other. There corresponds to this also a political transition period in which the state can be nothing but the revolutionary dictatorship of the proletariat."[75] Up to now this truth has been indisputable for socialists and it includes the recognition of the fact that the *state* will exist until victorious socialism develops into full communism. Engels's dictum about the *withering away* of the state is well known. We deliberately stressed, in the first thesis, that democracy is a form of state that will also wither away when the state withers away. And until our opponents replace Marxism by some sort of "non-state" viewpoint their arguments will constitute one big mistake.

Instead of speaking about the state (which *means*, about the demarcation of its *frontiers*!), they speak of a "socialist cultural zone", i.e., they deliberately choose an expression that is indefinite in the sense that all state questions are obliterated! Thus we get a ridiculous tautology: if there is no state there can, of course, be no question of frontiers. In that case the *whole* democratic-political programme is unnecessary. Nor will there be any republic, when the state "withers away".

The German chauvinist Lensch, in the articles we mentioned in Thesis 5 (footnote),* quoted an interesting passage from Engels's article "The Po and the Rhine". Amongst other things, Engels says in this article that in the course of historical development, which swallowed up a number of small and non-viable nations, the "frontiers of great and viable European nations" were being increasingly determined by the "language and sympathies" of the population. Engels calls these frontiers "natural".[76] Such was the case in the period of progressive capitalism in Europe, roughly from 1848 to 1871. Today, these democratically determined frontiers are more and more often being *broken down* by reactionary, imperialist capitalism. There is every sign that imperialism will leave its successor, socialism, a heritage of *less* democratic frontiers, a number of annexations in Europe and in other parts of the world. Is it to be supposed that victorious socialism, restoring and implementing full democracy all

---

* See this pamphlet, p. 117.—*Ed.*

along the line, will refrain from *democratically* demarcating state frontiers and ignore the "sympathies" of the population? These questions need only be stated to make it quite clear that our Polish colleagues are sliding down from Marxism towards imperialist Economism.

The old Economists, who made a caricature of Marxism, told the workers that "only the economic" was of importance to Marxists. The new Economists seem to think either that the democratic state of victorious socialism will exist without frontiers (like a "complex of sensations" without matter) or that frontiers will be delineated "only" in accordance with the needs of production. In actual fact its frontiers will be delineated democratically, i.e., in accordance with the will and "sympathies" of the population. Capitalism rides roughshod over these sympathies, adding more obstacles to the rapprochement of nations. Socialism, by organising production *without* class oppression, by ensuring the well-being of *all* members of the state, gives *full play* to the "sympathies" of the population, thereby promoting and greatly accelerating the drawing together and fusion of the nations.

To give the reader a rest from the heavy and clumsy Economism let us quote the reasoning of a socialist writer who is outside our dispute. That writer is Otto Bauer, who also has his own "pet little point"—"cultural and national autonomy"—but who argues quite correctly on a large number of most important questions. For example, in Chapter 29 of his book *The National Question and Social-Democracy*, he was doubly right in noting the use of national ideology to cover up *imperialist* policies. In Chapter 30, "Socialism and the Principle of Nationality", he says:

"The socialist community will never be able to include whole nations within its make-up by the use of force. Imagine the masses of the people, enjoying all the blessings of national culture, taking a full and active part in legislation and government, and, finally, supplied with arms—would it be possible to subordinate such a nation to the rule of an alien social organism by force? All state power rests on the force of arms. The present-day people's army, thanks to an ingenious mechanism, still constitutes a tool in the hands of a definite person, family or class exactly like the knightly and mercenary armies of the past. The army of the democratic community of a socialist society is nothing but the people armed, since it consists of highly cultured persons, working without compulsion in socialised workshops and taking full part in all spheres of political life. In such conditions any possibility of alien rule disappears."

This is true. It is *impossible* to abolish national (or any other political) oppression under capitalism, since this *requires* the abolition of classes, i.e., the introduction of socialism. But while being based on economics, socialism cannot be reduced to economics alone. A foundation—socialist production—is essential for the abolition of national oppression, but this foundation must *also* carry a democratically organised state, a democratic army, etc. By transforming capitalism into socialism the proletariat creates the *possibility* of abolishing national oppression; the possibility becomes *reality* "only"—"only"!—with the establishment of full democracy in all spheres, including the delineation of state frontiers in accordance with the "sympathies" of the population, including complete freedom to secede. And this, in turn, will serve as a basis for developing the *practical* elimination of even the slightest national friction and the least national mistrust, for an accelerated drawing together and fusion of nations that will be completed when the state *withers away*. This is the Marxist theory, the theory from which our Polish colleagues have mistakenly departed.

2. Is Democracy "Practicable" under Imperialism?

The old polemic conducted by Polish Social-Democrats against the self-determination of nations is based entirely on the argument that it is "impracticable" under capitalism. As long ago as 1903 we, the *Iskra* supporters, laughed at this argument in the Programme Commission of the Second Congress of the R.S.D.L.P., and said that it was a repetition of the distortion of Marxism preached by the (late lamented) Economists. In our theses we dealt with this error in particular detail and it is precisely on this point, which contains the theoretical kernel of the whole dispute, that the Polish comrades did not wish to (or could not?) answer *any* of our arguments.

To prove the economic impossibility of self-determination would require an economic analysis such as that used to prove the impracticability of prohibiting machines or introducing labour-money, etc. No one has even attempted to make such an analysis. No one will maintain that it has been possible to introduce "labour-money" under capitalism "by way of exception" in even one country, in the way it was possible for one small country to realise this impracticable self-determination, even without war or revolution, "by way of exception", in the era of the most rabid imperialism (Norway, 1905).

In general, political democracy is merely one of the possible *forms* of superstructure *above* capitalism (although it is theoretically the normal one for "pure" capitalism). The facts show that both capitalism and imperialism develop within the framework of *any* political form and subordinate them *all*. It is, therefore, a basic theoretical error to speak of the "impracticability" of *one* of the forms and of *one* of the demands of democracy.

The absence of an answer to these arguments from our Polish colleagues compels us to consider the discussion closed on this point. To make it graphic, so to say, we made the very concrete assertion that it would be "ridiculous" to deny the "practicability" of the restoration of Poland today, making it dependent on the strategic and other aspects of the present war. No reply was forthcoming!

The Polish comrades simply *repeated* an obviously incorrect assertion (§ II, 1), saying that "in questions of the annexation of foreign territories, forms of political democracy are pushed aside; sheer force is decisive. . . . Capital will never allow the people to decide the question of their state frontiers. . .". As though "capital" could "allow the people" to select *its* civil servants, the servants of imperialism! Or as though weighty decisions on important democratic questions, such as the establishment of a republic in place of a monarchy, or a militia in place of a regular army, were, *in general*, conceivable without "sheer force". Subjectively, the Polish comrades want to make Marxism "more profound" but they are doing it altogether unsuccessfully. *Objectively*, their phrases about impracticability are opportunism, because their tacit assumption is: this is "impracticable" without a series of revolutions, in the same way as democracy *as a whole*, *all* its demands taken together, is impracticable under imperialism.

Once only, at the very end of §II, 1, in the discussion on Alsace, our Polish colleagues abandoned the position of imperialist Economism and approached the question of one of the forms of democracy with a concrete answer and not with general references to the "economic". And it was precisely this approach that was wrong! It would, they wrote, be "particularist, undemocratic" if *some* Alsatians, without asking the French, were to "impose" on them a union with Alsace, although part of Alsace was German-orientated and this threatened war!!! The confusion is amusing: self-determination presumes (this is in itself clear, and we have given it special emphasis in our theses) freedom to *separate* from the oppressor state; but the fact that *union* with a state presumes the consent of *that state* is something that is "not customarily" mentioned in politics any more than the "consent" of a capitalist to receive profit or of a worker to receive wages is mentioned in economics! It is ridiculous even to speak of such a thing.

If one wants to be a Marxist politician, one should, in speaking of Alsace, attack the German socialist scoundrels for not fighting for Alsace's freedom to secede and attack the French socialist scoundrels for making their peace with the French bourgeoisie who want to annex the whole of Alsace by force—and both of them for serving the imperialism of "their own" country and for fearing a separate state, even if only a little one; the thing is to show *how* the socialists who recognise self-determination would solve the problem in a few weeks without going against the will of the Alsatians. To argue, instead, about the horrible danger of the French Alsatians "forcing" themselves on France is a real pearl.

3. What Is Annexation?

We raised this question in a most definite manner in our theses (Section 7).* The Polish comrades did *not* reply to it: they *evaded* it, insisting (1) that they are against annexations and explaining (2) why they are against them. It is true that these are very important questions. But they are questions of *another kind*. If we want our principles

---

* See this pamphlet, pp. 119-20.—*Ed.*

to be theoretically sound at all, if we want them to be clearly and precisely formulated, we cannot *evade* the question of what an annexation is, since this concept is used in our political propaganda and agitation. The evasion of the question in a discussion between colleagues cannot be interpreted as anything but desertion of one's position.

Why have we raised this question? We explained this when we raised it. It is because "a protest against annexations is nothing but recognition of the right to self-determination". The concept of annexation usually includes: (1) the concept of force (joining by means of force); (2) the concept of oppression by another nation (the joining of "*alien*" regions, etc.), and, sometimes (3) the concept of violation of the *status quo*. We pointed this out in the theses and this did not meet with any criticism.

Can Social-Democrats be against the use of force in general, it may be asked? Obviously not. This means that we are against annexations not because they constitute force, but for some other reason. Nor can the Social-Democrats be for the *status quo*. However you may twist and turn, annexation is *violation of the self-determination* of a nation, it is the establishment of state *frontiers contrary to the will of the population*.

To be against annexations *means* to be in favour of the right to self-determination. To be "against the forcible retention of any nation within the frontiers of a given state" (we deliberately employed this slightly changed formulation of the same idea in Section 4 of our theses,* and the Polish comrades *answered* us with *complete* clarity at the beginning of their § I, 4, that they "are against the forcible retention of oppressed nations within the frontiers of the annexing state")—is *the same* as being in favour of the self-determination of nations.

We do not want to haggle over words. If there is a party that says in its programme (or in a resolution binding on all—the form does not matter) that it is against annexations,** against the forcible retention of oppressed

---

* See this pamphlet, pp. 114-15.—*Ed.*
** Karl Radek formulated this as "against old and new annexations" in one of his articles in *Berner Tagwacht*.

nations within the frontiers of *its* state, we declare our complete agreement in principle with that party. It would be absurd to insist on the *word* "self-determination". And if there are people in our Party who want to change *words* in this spirit, who want to amend Clause 9 of our Party Programme, we should consider our differences with *such* comrades to be anything but a matter of principle!

The only thing that matters is political clarity and theoretical soundness of our slogans.

In verbal discussions on this question—the importance of which nobody will deny, especially now, in view of the war—we have met the following argument (we have not come across it in the press): *a protest against* a known evil does not necessarily mean recognition of a positive concept that precludes the evil. This is obviously an unfounded argument and, apparently, as such has not been reproduced in the press. If a socialist party declares that it is "against the forcible retention of an oppressed nation within the frontiers of the annexing state", it is *thereby committed to renounce retention by force* when it comes to power.

We do not for one moment doubt that if Hindenburg were to accomplish the semi-conquest of Russia tomorrow and this semi-conquest were to be expressed by the appearance of a new Polish state (in connection with the desire of Britain and France to weaken tsarism somewhat), something that is quite "practicable" from the standpoint of the economic laws of capitalism and imperialism, and if, the day after tomorrow, the socialist revolution were to be victorious in Petrograd, Berlin and Warsaw, the Polish socialist government, like the Russian and German socialist governments, would renounce the "forcible retention" of, say, the Ukrainians, "within the frontiers of the Polish state". If there were members of the *Gazeta Robotnicza* Editorial Board in that government they would no doubt sacrifice their "theses", thereby disproving the "theory" that "the right of self-determination is not applicable to a socialist society". If we thought otherwise we should not put a comradely discussion with the Polish Social-Democrats on the agenda but would rather conduct a ruthless struggle against them as chauvinists.

Suppose I were to go out into the streets of any European city and make a public "protest", which I then published in the press, against my not being permitted to purchase a man as a slave. There is no doubt that people would have the right to regard me as a slave-owner, a champion of the principle, or system, if you like of slavery. No one would be fooled by the fact that my sympathies with slavery were expressed in the negative form of a protest and not in a positive form ("I am for slavery"). A political "protest" is *quite* the equivalent of a political programme; this is so obvious that one feels rather awkward at having to explain it. In any case, we are firmly convinced that on the part of the Zimmerwald Left, at any rate—we do not speak of the Zimmerwald group as a whole since it contains Martov and other Kautskyites— we shall not meet with any "protest" if we say that in the Third International there will be no place for people capable of separating a political protest from a political programme, of counterposing the one to the other, etc.

Not wishing to haggle over words, we take the liberty of expressing the sincere hope that the Polish Social-Democrats will try soon to formulate, officially, their proposal to delete Clause 9 from our Party Programme (which is also *theirs*) and also from the Programme of the International (the resolution of the 1896 London Congress), as well as *their own* definition of the relevant political concepts of "old and new annexations" and of "the forcible retention of an oppressed nation within the frontiers of the annexing state".

Let us now turn to the next question.

4. For or Against Annexations?

In § 3 of Part One of their theses the Polish comrades declare very definitely that they are against any kind of annexation. Unfortunately, in § 4 of the same part we find an assertion that must be considered annexationist. It opens with the following ... how can it be put more delicately?... the following strange phrase:

"The starting-point of Social-Democracy's struggle against annexations, against the forcible retention of oppressed nations within the frontiers of the annexing state is *renunciation of any defence of the fatherland* [the authors' italics], which, in the era of imperialism, is defence of the rights of one's own bourgeoisie to oppress and plunder foreign peoples...."

What's this? How is it put?

"The starting-point of the struggle against annexations is renunciation of *any* defence of the fatherland...." But any national war and any national revolt can be called "defence of the fatherland" and, until now, has been *generally* recognised as such! We are against annexations, *but* ... we mean by this that we are against the annexed waging a war *for* their liberation from those who have annexed them, that we are against the annexed revolting to liberate themselves from those who have annexed them! Isn't that an annexationist declaration?

The authors of the theses motivate their ... strange assertion by saying that "in the era of imperialism" defence of the fatherland amounts to defence of the right of one's own bourgeoisie to oppress foreign peoples. This, however, is true *only* in respect of an imperialist war, i.e., in respect of a war *between* imperialist powers or groups of powers, when *both* belligerents not only oppress "foreign peoples" but are fighting a war *to decide* who shall have a *greater share* in oppressing foreign peoples!

The authors seem to present the question of "defence of the fatherland" very differently from the way it is presented by our Party. We renounce "defence of the fatherland" in an *imperialist* war. This is said as clearly as it can be in the Manifesto of our Party's Central Committee and in the Berne resolutions* reprinted in the pamphlet *Socialism and War*, which has been published both in German and French. We stressed this *twice* in our theses (footnotes to Sections 4 and 6).** The authors of the Polish theses seem to renounce defence of the fatherland *in general*, i.e., *for a national war as well*, believing, perhaps, that in the "era of imperialism" national wars *are impossible*. We say "perhaps" because the Polish comrades have *not* expressed this view in their theses.

Such a view is clearly expressed in the theses of the German *Internationale* group[77] and in the Junius[78] pam-

---

* See V. I. Lenin, *Collected Works*, Vol. 21, pp. 25-34, 158-64.—*Ed.*
** See this pamphlet, pp. 116, 118.—*Ed.*

phlet which is dealt with in a special article.* In addition to what is said there, let us note that the national revolt of an annexed region or country against the annexing country may be called precisely a revolt and not a war (we have heard this objection made and, therefore, cite it here, although we do not think this terminological dispute a serious one). In any case, hardly anybody would risk denying that annexed Belgium, Serbia, Galicia and Armenia would call their "revolt" against those who annexed them "defence of the fatherland" *and would do so in all justice*. It looks as if the Polish comrades are *against* this type of revolt on the grounds that there is *also* a bourgeoisie in these annexed countries which *also* oppresses foreign peoples or, more exactly, could oppress them, since the question is one of the "*right* to oppress". Consequently, the given war or revolt is not assessed on the strength of its *real* social content (the struggle of an oppressed nation for its liberation from the oppressor nation) but the possible exercise of the "*right* to oppress" by a bourgeoisie which is at present itself oppressed. If Belgium, let us say, is annexed by Germany in 1917, and in 1918 revolts to secure her liberation, the Polish comrades will be against her revolt on the grounds that the Belgian bourgeoisie possess "the right to oppress foreign peoples"!

There is nothing Marxist or even revolutionary in this argument. If we do not want to betray socialism we *must* support *every* revolt against our chief enemy, the bourgeoisie of the big states, provided it is not the revolt of a reactionary class. By refusing to support the revolt of annexed regions we become, objectively, annexationists. It is precisely in the "era of imperialism", which is the era of nascent social revolution, that the proletariat will today give especially vigorous support to any revolt of the annexed regions so that tomorrow, or simultaneously, it may attack the bourgeoisie of the "great" power that is weakened by the revolt.

The Polish comrades, however, go further in their annexationism. They are not only against any revolt by the annexed regions; they are against *any* restoration of their independence, even a peaceful one! Listen to this:

---

* See V. I. Lenin, *Collected Works*, Vol. 22, pp. 305-19.—*Ed.*

"Social-Democracy, rejecting all responsibility for the consequences of the policy of oppression pursued by imperialism, and conducting the sharpest struggle against them, *does not by any means favour the erection of new frontier posts in Europe or the re-erection of those swept away by imperialism*" (the authors' italics).

Today "imperialism has swept away the frontier posts" between Germany and Belgium and between Russia and Galicia. International Social-Democracy, if you please, ought to be against their re-erection in general, whatever the means. In 1905, "in the era of imperialism", when Norway's autonomous Diet proclaimed her secession from Sweden, and Sweden's war against Norway, as preached by the Swedish reactionaries, did not take place, what with the resistance of the Swedish workers and the international imperialist situation—Social-Democracy ought to have been against Norway's secession, since it undoubtedly meant "the erection of new frontier posts in Europe"!!

This is downright annexationism. There is no need to refute it because it refutes itself. No socialist party would risk taking this stand: "We oppose annexations in general but we sanction annexations for Europe or tolerate them once they have been made"....

We need deal only with the theoretical sources of the error that has led our Polish comrades to such a patent... "impossibility". We shall say further on why there is no reason to make exceptions for "Europe". The following two phrases from the theses will explain the other sources of the error:

"Wherever the wheel of imperialism has rolled over and crushed an already formed capitalist state, the political and economic concentration of the capitalist world, paving the way for socialism, takes place in the brutal form of imperialist oppression ...."

This justification of annexations is not Marxism but Struveism. Russian Social-Democrats who remember the 1890s in Russia have a good knowledge of this manner of distorting Marxism, which is common to Struve, Cunow, Legien and Co. In another of the theses (II, 3) of the Polish comrades we read the following, specifically about the German Struveists, the so-called "social-imperialists":

(The slogan of self-determination) "provides the social-imperialists with an opportunity, by demonstrating the illusory nature of that slogan, to represent our struggle against national oppression as historically unfounded sentimentality, thereby undermining the faith of the proletariat in the scientific validity of the Social-Democratic programme...."

This means that the authors consider the position of the German Struveists "scientific"! Our congratulations.

One "trifle", however, brings down this amazing argument which threatens to show that the Lensches, Cunows and Parvuses are *right* in comparison to us: it is that the Lensches are consistent people in their own way and in issue No. 8-9 of the chauvinist German *Glocke*— we deliberately quoted it in our theses—Lensch demonstrates *simultaneously* both the "scientific invalidity" of the self-determination slogan (the Polish Social-Democrats apparently believe that *this* argument of Lensch's is irrefutable, as can be seen from their arguments in the theses we have quoted) *and* the "scientific invalidity" of the slogan against annexations!!

For Lensch had an excellent understanding of that simple truth which we pointed out to those Polish colleagues who showed no desire to reply to our statement: there is no difference "either political or economic", or even logical, between the "recognition" of self-determination and the "protest" against annexations. If the Polish comrades regard the arguments of the Lensches against self-determination to be irrefutable, there is one *fact* that has to be accepted: the Lensches also use *all* these arguments to oppose the struggle against annexations.

The theoretical error that underlies all the arguments of our Polish colleagues has led them to the point of becoming *inconsistent annexationists*.

5. Why Are Social-Democrats Against Annexations?

In our view the answer is obvious: because annexation violates the self-determination of nations, or, in other words, is a form of national oppression.

In the view of the Polish Social-Democrats there have to be *special* explanations of why we are against annexations, and it is these (I, 3 in the theses) that inevitably enmesh the authors in a further series of contradictions.

They produce two reasons to "justify" our opposition

to annexations (the "scientifically valid" arguments of the Lensches notwithstanding):

First:

"To the assertion that annexations in Europe are essential for the military security of a victorious imperialist state, the Social-Democrats counterpose the fact that annexations only serve to sharpen antagonisms, thereby increasing the danger of war...."

This is an inadequate reply to the Lensches because their chief argument is not that annexations are a military necessity but that they are *economically* progressive and under imperialism mean concentration. Where is the logic if the Polish Social-Democrats in the same breath recognise the progressive nature of *such* a concentration, refusing to re-erect frontier posts in Europe that have been swept away by imperialism, and protest *against* annexations?

Furthermore, the danger of *what* wars is increased by annexations? Not imperialist wars, because they have other causes; the chief antagonisms in the present imperialist war are undoubtedly those between Germany and Britain, and between Germany and Russia. These antagonisms have nothing to do with annexations. It is the danger of *national* wars and national revolts that is increased. But how can one declare national wars to be *impossible* in "the era of imperialism", on the one hand, and then speak of the "danger" of national wars, on the other? This is not logical. The second argument:

Annexations "create a gulf between the proletariat of the ruling nation and that of the oppressed nation ... the proletariat of the oppressed nation would unite with its bourgeoisie and regard the proletariat of the ruling nation as its enemy. Instead of the proletariat waging an international class struggle against the international bourgeoisie it would be split and ideologically corrupted...".

We fully agree with these arguments. But is it logical to put forward simultaneously two arguments on the same question which cancel each other out. In §3 of the first part of the theses we find the above arguments that regard annexations as causing a *split* in the proletariat, and next to it, in § 4, we are told that we must oppose the annulment of annexations already effected in Europe and favour "the education of the working masses of the oppressed and the oppressor nations in a spirit of solidarity in struggle". If the annulment of annexations is reactionary "sentimentality", annexations *must not* be said to create a "gulf" between sections of the "proletariat" and cause a "split", but should, on the contrary, be regarded as a condition for the *bringing together* of the proletariat of different nations.

We say: In order that we may have the strength to accomplish the socialist revolution and overthrow the bourgeoisie, the workers must unite more closely and this close union is promoted by the struggle for self-determination, i.e., the struggle against annexations. We are consistent. But the Polish comrades who say that European annexations are "non-annullable" and national wars, "impossible", defeat themselves by contending "against" annexations with the use of arguments *about* national wars! These arguments are to the effect that annexations *hamper* the drawing together and fusion of workers of different nations!

In other words, the Polish Social-Democrats, in order to contend against annexations, have to draw for arguments on the theoretical stock *they themselves* reject in principle.

The question of colonies makes this even more obvious.

6. Is It Right to Contrast "Europe" with the Colonies in the Present Question?

Our theses say that the demand for the immediate liberation of the colonies is as "impracticable" (that is, it cannot be effected without a number of revolutions and is not stable without socialism) under capitalism as the self-determination of nations, the election of civil servants by the people, the democratic republic, and so on—and, furthermore, that the demand for the liberation of the colonies is nothing more than "the recognition of the right of nations to self-determination".

The Polish comrades have not answered a single one of these arguments. They have tried to differentiate between "Europe" and the colonies. For Europe alone they become inconsistent annexationists by refusing to annul any annexations once these have been made. As for the colonies, they demand unconditionally: "Get out of the colonies!"

Russian socialists must put forward the demand: "Get out of Turkestan, Khiva, Bukhara, etc.", but, it is alleged, they would be guilty of "utopianism", "unscientific sentimentality" and so on if they demanded a similar freedom of secession for Poland, Finland, the Ukraine, etc. British socialists must demand: "Get out of Africa, India, Australia", but not out of Ireland. What are the theoretical grounds for a distinction that is so patently false? This question cannot be evaded.

The chief "ground" of those opposed to self-determination is its "impracticability". The same idea, with a nuance, is expressed in the reference to "economic and political concentration".

Obviously, concentration *also* comes about with the annexation of colonies. There was formerly an economic distinction between the colonies and the European peoples—at least, the majority of the latter—the colonies having been drawn into *commodity* exchange but not into capitalist *production*. Imperialism changed this. Imperialism is, among other things, the export of *capital*. Capitalist production is being transplanted to the colonies at an ever increasing rate. They cannot be extricated from dependence on European finance capital. From the military standpoint, as well as from the standpoint of expansion, the separation of the colonies is practicable, as a general rule, only under socialism; under capitalism it is practicable only by way of exception or at the cost of a series of revolts and revolutions both in the colonies and the metropolitan countries.

The greater part of the dependent nations in Europe are capitalistically more developed than the colonies (though not all, the exceptions being the Albanians and many non-Russian peoples in Russia). But it is just this that generates greater resistance to national oppression and annexations! Precisely because of this, the development of capitalism is *more secure* in Europe under any political conditions, including those of separation, than in the colonies.... "There," the Polish comrades say about the colonies (I, 4), "capitalism is still confronted with the task

of developing the productive forces independently...."
This is even more noticeable in Europe: capitalism is undoubtedly developing the productive forces more vigorously, rapidly and independently in Poland, Finland, the Ukraine and Alsace than in India, Turkestan, Egypt and other straightforward colonies. In a commodity-producing society, no independent development, or development of any sort whatsoever, is possible without capital. In Europe the dependent nations have both *their own* capital and easy access to it on a wide range of terms. The colonies have no capital of *their own*, or none to speak of, and under finance capital no colony can obtain any except on terms of political submission. What then, in face of all this, is the significance of the demand to liberate the colonies immediately and unconditionally? Is it not clear that it is more "utopian" in the vulgar, caricature-"Marxist" sense of the word, "utopian" in the sense in which it is used by the Struves, Lensches, Cunows, with the Polish comrades unfortunately following in their footsteps? Any deviation from the ordinary, the commonplace, as well as everything that is revolutionary, is here labelled "utopianism". But revolutionary movements of *all* kinds—including national movements—are more possible, more practicable, more stubborn, more conscious and more difficult to defeat in Europe than they are in the colonies.

Socialism, say the Polish comrades (I, 3), "will be able to give the underdeveloped peoples of the colonies *unselfish cultural aid without ruling* over them". This is perfectly true. But what grounds are there for supposing that a great nation, a great state that goes over to socialism, will not be able to attract a small, oppressed European nation by means of "unselfish cultural aid"? It is the freedom to secede *"granted"* to the colonies by the Polish Social-Democrats that will attract the small but cultured and politically *exacting* oppressed nations of Europe to union with great socialist states, because under socialism a great state will mean so many hours *less* work a day and so much more *pay* a day. The masses of working people, as they liberate themselves from the bourgeois yoke, *will gravitate* irresistibly towards union and integration with the great, advanced socialist nations for the sake of that "cultural aid", provided yesterday's oppressors do not infringe on the long-oppressed nations' highly developed democratic feeling of self-respect, and provided they are granted equality in everything, including state construction, that is, experience in organising "their own" state. Under capitalism this "experience" means war, isolation, seclusion, and the narrow egoism of the small privileged nations (Holland, Switzerland). Under socialism the working people themselves will nowhere consent to seclusion merely for the above-mentioned purely economic motives, while the variety of political forms, freedom to secede, and experience in state organisation—there will be all this until the state in all its forms withers away—will be the basis of a prosperous cultured life and an earnest that the nations will draw closer together and integrate at an ever faster pace.

By setting the colonies aside and contrasting them to Europe the Polish comrades step into a contradiction which immediately brings down the whole of their fallacious argument.

7. Marxism or Proudhonism?

By way of an exception, our Polish comrades parry our reference to Marx's attitude towards the separation of Ireland directly and not indirectly. What is their objection? References to Marx's position from 1848 to 1871, they say, are "not of the slightest value". The argument advanced in support of this unusually irate and peremptory assertion is that "at one and the same time" Marx opposed the strivings for independence of the "Czechs, South Slavs, etc."[79]

The argument is so very irate because it is so very unsound. According to the Polish Marxists, Marx was simply a muddlehead who "in one breath" said contradictory things! This is altogether untrue, and it is certainly not Marxism. It is precisely the demand for "concrete" analysis, which our Polish comrades insist on, but do not themselves apply, that makes it necessary for us to investigate whether Marx's different attitudes towards different concrete "national" movements did not spring from one and the same socialist outlook.

Marx is known to have favoured Polish independence in the interests of *European* democracy in its struggle against the power and influence—or, it might be said, against the omnipotence and predominating reactionary influence—of tsarism. That this attitude was correct was most clearly and practically demonstrated in 1849, when the Russian serf army crushed the national liberation and revolutionary-democratic rebellion in Hungary. From that time until Marx's death, and even later, until 1890, when there was a danger that tsarism, allied with France, would wage a reactionary war against a *non-imperialist* and nationally independent Germany, Engels stood first and foremost for a struggle against tsarism. It was for this reason, and exclusively for this reason, that Marx and Engels were opposed to the national movement of the Czechs and South Slavs. A simple reference to what Marx and Engels wrote in 1848 and 1849 will prove to anyone who is interested in Marxism in real earnest and not merely for the purpose of brushing Marxism aside, that Marx and Engels at that time drew a clear and definite *distinction* between "whole reactionary nations" serving as "Russian outposts" in Europe, and "revolutionary nations", namely, the Germans, Poles and Magyars. This is a fact. And it was indicated *at the time with incontrovertible* truth: in 1848 revolutionary nations fought for liberty, whose principal enemy was tsarism, whereas the Czechs, etc., were in fact reactionary nations, and outposts of tsarism.

What is the lesson to be drawn from this concrete example which must be analysed *concretely* if there is any desire to be true to Marxism? Only this: (1) that the interests of the liberation of a number of big and very big nations in Europe rate higher than the interests of the movement for liberation of small nations; (2) that the demand for democracy must not be considered in isolation but on a European—today we should say a world—scale.

That is all there is to it. There is no hint of any repudiation of that elementary socialist principle which the Poles forget but to which Marx was *always* faithful—that no nation can be free if it oppresses other nations. If the concrete situation which confronted Marx when tsarism dominated international politics were to repeat itself, for instance, in the form of a few nations starting a socialist revolution (as a bourgeois-democratic revolution was started in Europe in 1848), and *other* nations serving as the chief bulwarks of bourgeois reaction—then we too would have to be in favour of a revolutionary war against the latter, in favour of "crushing" them, in favour of destroying all their outposts, no matter what small-nation movements arose in them. Consequently, instead of rejecting any examples of Marx's tactics—this would mean professing Marxism while abandoning it in practice—we must analyse them concretely and draw invaluable lessons for the future. The several demands of democracy, including self-determination, are not an absolute, but only a *small part* of the general-democratic (now: general-socialist) *world* movement. In individual concrete cases, the part may contradict the whole; if so, it must be rejected. It is possible that the republican movement in one country may be merely an instrument of the clerical or financial-monarchist intrigues of other countries; if so, we must *not* support this particular, concrete movement, but it would be ridiculous to delete the demand for a republic from the programme of international Social-Democracy on these grounds.

In what way has the concrete situation changed between the periods of 1848-71 and 1898-1916 (I take the most important landmarks of imperialism as a period: from the Spanish-American imperialist war to the European imperialist war)? Tsarism has manifestly and indisputably ceased to be the chief mainstay of reaction, first, because it is supported by international finance capital, particularly French, and, secondly, because of 1905. At that time the system of big national states—the democracies of Europe—was bringing democracy and socialism to the world in spite of tsarism.* Marx and Engels did not live to

---

* Ryazanov has published in Grünberg's *Archives of the History of Socialism* (1916, I) a very interesting article by Engels on the Polish question, written in 1866. Engels emphasises that the proletariat must recognise the political independence and "self-determination" ("right to dispose of itself" [These words are in English in the original.—*Ed.*]) of the great, major nations of Europe, and points to the absurdity of the "principle of nationalities" (particularly in its Bonapartist application), i.e., of placing any small nation on the same level as these big ones. "And as to Russia," says Engels, "she could only be mentioned

see the period of imperialism. The system now is a handful of imperialist "Great" Powers (five or six in number), each oppressing other nations: and this oppression is a source for artificially retarding the collapse of capitalism, and artificially supporting opportunism and social-chauvinism in the imperialist nations ·which dominate the world. At that time, West-European democracy, liberating the big nations, was opposed to tsarism, which used certain small-nation movements for reactionary ends. Today, the socialist proletariat, split into chauvinists, "social-imperialists", on the one hand, and revolutionaries, on the other, is confronted by an *alliance* of tsarist imperialism and advanced capitalist, European, imperialism, which is based on their common oppression of a number of nations.

Such are the concrete changes that have taken place in the situation, and it is just these that the Polish Social-Democrats ignore, in spite of their promise to be concrete! Hence the concrete change in the *application* of the same socialist principles: *formerly* the main thing was to fight "against tsarism" (and against certain small-nation movements that *it* was using for undemocratic ends), and for the greater revolutionary peoples of the West; the main thing *today* is to stand against the united, aligned front of the imperialist powers, the imperialist bourgeoisie and the social-imperialists, and *for* the utilisation of *all* national movements against imperialism for the purposes of the socialist revolution. The *more purely* proletarian the struggle against the general imperialist front now is, the more vital, obviously, is the internationalist principle: "No nation can be free if it oppresses other nations."

In the name of their doctrinaire concept of social revolution, the Proudhonists ignored the international role of Poland and brushed aside the national movements. Equally doctrinaire is the attitude of the Polish Social-Democrats, who *break up* the international front of struggle against the social-imperialists, and (objectively) help the latter by their vacillations on the question of annexations.

---

as the detainer of an immense amount of stolen property [i.e., oppressed nations] which would have to be disgorged on the day of reckoning."[80] Both Bonapartism and tsarism *utilise* the small-nation movements for *their own* benefit, *against* European democracy.

For it is precisely the international front of proletarian struggle that has changed in relation to the concrete position of the small nations: at that time (1848-71) the small nations were important as the potential allies either of "Western democracy" and the revolutionary nations, or of tsarism; now (1898-1914) that is no longer so; today they are important as one of the nutritive media of the parasitism and, consequently, the social-imperialism of the "dominant nations". The important thing is not whether one-fiftieth or one-hundredth of the small nations are liberated before the socialist revolution, but the fact that in the epoch of imperialism, owing to objective causes, the proletariat has been split into two international camps, one of which has been corrupted by the crumbs that fall from the table of the dominant-nation bourgeoisie—obtained, among other things, from the double or triple exploitation of small nations—while the other cannot liberate itself without liberating the small nations, without educating the masses in an anti-chauvinist, i.e., anti-annexationist, i.e., "self-determinationist", spirit.

This, the most important aspect of the question, is ignored by our Polish comrades, who do *not* view things from the key position in the epoch of imperialism, the standpoint of the division of the international proletariat into two camps.

Here are some other concrete examples of their Proudhonism: (1) their attitude to the Irish rebellion of 1916, of which later; (2) the declaration in the theses (II, 3, end of § 3) that the slogan of socialist revolution "must not be overshadowed by anything". The idea that the slogan of socialist revolution can be "overshadowed" by *linking* it up with a consistently revolutionary position on all questions, including the national question, is certainly profoundly anti-Marxist.

The Polish Social-Democrats consider our programme "national-reformist". Compare these two practical proposals: (1) for autonomy (Polish theses, III, 4), and (2) for freedom to secede. It is in this, and in this alone, that our programmes differ! And is it not clear that it is precisely the first programme that is reformist and not the second? A reformist change is one which leaves intact the foundations of the power of the ruling class and is merely a concession leaving its power unimpaired. A revolutionary change undermines the foundations of power. A reformist national programme does *not* abolish *all* the privileges of the ruling nation; it does *not* establish complete equality; it does *not* abolish national oppression *in all its forms*. An "autonomous" nation does not enjoy rights equal to those of the "ruling" nation; our Polish comrades could not have failed to notice this had they not (like our old Economists) obstinately avoided making an analysis of *political* concepts and categories. Until 1905 autonomous Norway, as a part of Sweden, enjoyed the widest autonomy, but she was not Sweden's equal. Only by her free secession was her equality manifested *in practice* and proved (and let us add in parenthesis that it was this free secession that created the basis for a more intimate and more democratic association, founded on equality of rights). As long as Norway was merely autonomous, the Swedish aristocracy had *one* additional privilege; and secession did not "mitigate" this privilege (the essence of reformism lies in *mitigating* an evil and not in destroying it), but *eliminated* it *altogether* (the principal criterion of the revolutionary character of a programme).

Incidentally, autonomy, as a reform, differs in principle from freedom to secede, as a revolutionary measure. This is unquestionable. But as everyone knows, in practice a reform is often merely a step towards revolution. It is autonomy that enables a nation forcibly retained within the boundaries of a given state to crystallise into a nation, to gather, assess and organise its forces, and to select the most opportune moment for a *declaration* ... in the "Norwegian" spirit: We, the autonomous diet of such-and-such a nation, or of such-and-such a territory, declare that the Emperor of all the Russias has ceased to be King of Poland, etc. The usual "objection" to this is that such questions are decided by wars and not by declarations. True: in the vast majority of cases they are decided by wars (just as questions of the form of government of big states are decided, in the vast majority of cases, only by wars and revolutions). However, it would do no harm to reflect whether *such* an "objection" to the political programme of a revolutionary party is logical. Are we opposed to wars and revolutions *for* what is just and beneficial to the proletariat, *for* democracy and socialism?

"But we cannot be in favour of a war between great nations, in favour of the slaughter of twenty million people for the sake of the problematical liberation of a small nation with a population of perhaps ten or twenty millions!" Of course not! And it does not mean that we throw complete national equality out of our Programme; it means that the democratic interests of *one* country must be subordinated to the democratic interests of *several and all* countries. Let us assume that between two great monarchies there is a little monarchy whose kinglet is "bound" by blood and other ties to the monarchs of both neighbouring countries. Let us further assume that the declaration of a republic in the little country and the expulsion of *its* monarch would in practice lead to a war between the two neighbouring big countries for the restoration of that or another monarch in the little country. There is no doubt that all international Social-Democracy, as well as the really internationalist section of Social-Democracy in the little country, *would be against substituting a republic for the monarchy* in this case. The substitution of a republic for a monarchy is not an absolute, but one of the democratic demands, subordinate to the interests of democracy (and still more, of course, to those of the socialist proletariat) as a whole. A case like this would in all probability not give rise to the slightest disagreement among Social-Democrats in any country. But if any Social-Democrat were to propose on *these* grounds that the demand for a republic be deleted altogether from the programme of international Social-Democracy, he would certainly be regarded as quite mad. He would be told that after all one must not forget the elementary logical difference between the *general* and the *particular*.

This example brings us, from a somewhat different angle, to the question of the *internationalist* education of the working class. Can such education—on the necessity and urgent importance of which differences of opinion among the Zimmerwald Left are inconceivable—be *concretely identical* in great, oppressor nations and in small, oppressed nations, in annexing nations and in annexed nations?

Obviously not. The way to the common goal—complete equality, the closest association and the eventual *amalgamation of all* nations—obviously runs along different routes in each concrete case, as, let us say, the way to a point in the centre of this page runs left from one edge and right, from the opposite edge. If a Social-Democrat from a great, oppressing, annexing nation, while advocating the amalgamation of nations in general, were for one moment to forget that "his" Nicholas II, "his" Wilhelm, George, Poincaré, etc., *also stand for amalgamation* with small nations (by means of annexations)—Nicholas II for "amalgamation" with Galicia, Wilhelm II for "amalgamation" with Belgium, etc.—such a Social-Democrat would be a ridiculous doctrinaire in theory and an abettor of imperialism in practice.

In the internationalist education of the workers of the oppressor countries, emphasis must necessarily be laid on their advocating freedom for the oppressed countries to secede and their fighting for it. Without this there can be *no* internationalism. It is our right and duty to treat every Social-Democrat of an oppressor nation who *fails* to conduct such propaganda as a scoundrel and an imperialist. This is an absolute demand, even where the *chance* of secession being possible and "practicable" before the introduction of socialism is only one in a thousand.

It is our duty to teach the workers to be "indifferent" to national distinctions. There is no doubt about that. But it must not be the indifference of the *annexationists*. A member of an oppressor nation must be "indifferent" to whether small nations belong to *his* state *or to a neighbouring* state, or to themselves, according to where their sympathies lie: without such "indifference" he is *not* a Social-Democrat. To be an internationalist Social-Democrat one must *not* think only of one's own nation, but place *above it* the interests of all nations, their common liberty and equality. Everyone accepts this in "theory" but displays an annexationist indifference in practice. There is the root of the evil.

On the other hand, a Social-Democrat from a small nation must emphasise in his agitation the *second* word of our general formula: "voluntary *integration*" of nations. He may, without failing in his duties as an internationalist, be in favour of *both* the political independence of his nation and its integration with the neighbouring state of X, Y, Z, etc. But in all cases he must fight *against* small-nation narrow-mindedness, seclusion and isolation, consider the whole and the general, subordinate the particular to the general interest.

People who have not gone into the question thoroughly think that it is "contradictory" for the Social-Democrats of oppressor nations to insist on the "freedom to *secede*", while Social-Democrats of oppressed nations insist on the "freedom to *integrate*". However, a little reflection will show that there is not, and cannot be, any *other* road to internationalism and the amalgamation of nations, any other road *from the given* situation to this goal.

And now we come to the *specific* position of Dutch and Polish Social-Democrats.

8. The Specific and the General in the Position of the Dutch and Polish Social-Democrat Internationalists

There is not the slightest doubt that the Dutch and Polish Marxists who oppose self-determination are among the best revolutionary and internationalist elements in international Social-Democracy. How *can* it be then that their theoretical arguments as we have seen, are a mass of errors? There is not a single correct general argument, nothing but imperialist Economism!

It is not at all due to the especially bad subjective qualities of the Dutch and Polish comrades but to the *specific* objective conditions in their countries. Both countries are: (1) small and helpless in the present-day "system" of great powers; (2) both are geographically situated between tremendously powerful imperialist plunderers engaged in the most bitter rivalry with each other (Britain and Germany; Germany and Russia); (3) in both there are terribly strong memories and traditions of the times when they *themselves* were great powers: Holland was once a colonial power greater than England, Poland was more cultured and was a stronger great power than Russia and Prussia; (4) to this day both retain their privileges consisting in the oppression of other peoples: the Dutch bourgeois owns the very wealthy Dutch East Indies; the Polish landed proprietor oppresses the Ukrainian and Byelorussian peasant; the Polish bourgeois, the Jew, etc.

The particularity comprised in the combination of these four points is not to be found in Ireland, Portugal (she was at one time annexed to Spain), Alsace, Norway, Finland, the Ukraine, the Lettish and Byelorussian territories or many others. And it is this very peculiarity that is the *real essence* of the matter! When the Dutch and Polish Social-Democrats reason against self-determination, using *general* arguments, i.e., those that concern imperialism in general, socialism in general, democracy in general, national oppression in general, we may truly say that they wallow in mistakes. But one has only to discard this obviously erroneous *shell* of general arguments and examine the *essence* of the question from the standpoint of the *specific* conditions obtaining in Holland and Poland for their particular position to become *comprehensible* and quite legitimate. It may be said, without any fear of sounding paradoxical, that when the Dutch and Polish Marxists battle against self-determination they do not say quite what they mean, or, to put it another way, mean quite what they say.*

We have already quoted one example in our theses.** Gorter is against the self-determination of *his own* country but *in favour* of self-determination for the Dutch East Indies, oppressed as they are by "his" nation! Is it any wonder that we see in him a more sincere internationalist and a fellow-thinker who is closer to us than those who recognise self-determination *as* verbally and hypocritically as Kautsky in Germany, and Trotsky and Martov in Russia? The general and fundamental principles of Marxism undoubtedly imply the duty to struggle for the freedom to secede for nations that are oppressed by "one's own" nation, but they certainly do not require the independence specifically of Holland to be made a matter of paramount

---

* Let us recall that *all* the Polish Social-Democrats *recognised* self-determination *in general* in their Zimmerwald declaration, although their formulation was slightly different.
** See this pamphlet, p. 118.—*Ed.*

importance—Holland, which suffers most from her narrow, callous, selfish and stultifying seclusion: let the whole world burn, we stand aside from it all, "we" are satisfied with our old spoils and the rich "left-overs", the Indies, "we" are not concerned with anything else!

Here is another example. Karl Radek, a Polish Social-Democrat, who has done particularly great service by his determined struggle for internationalism in German Social-Democracy since the outbreak of war, made a furious attack on self-determination in an article entitled "The Right of Nations to Self-Determination" (*Lichtstrahlen*[81]—a Left Radical monthly prohibited by the Prussian censor, edited by J. Borchardt—1915, December 5, Third Year of Publication, No. 3). He quotes, incidentally, *only* Dutch and Polish authorities in his support and propounds, amongst others, the argument that self-determination fosters the idea that "it is allegedly the duty of Social-Democrats to support any struggle for independence".

From the standpoint of *general* theory this argument is outrageous, because it is clearly illogical: first, no democratic demand can fail to give rise to abuses, unless the specific is subordinated to the general; we are not obliged to support either "any" struggle for independence or "any" republican or anti-clerical movement. Secondly, *no* formula for the struggle against national oppression can fail to suffer from the *same* "shortcoming". Radek himself in *Berner Tagwacht*[82] used the formula (1915, Issue 253): "Against old and new annexations." Any Polish nationalist will legitimately "deduce" from this formula: "Poland is an annexment, I am against annexations, *i.e.*, I am for the independence of Poland." Or I recall Rosa Luxemburg saying in an article written in 1908,[83] that the formula: "against national oppression" was quite adequate. But any Polish nationalist would say—*and quite justly*—that annexation is *one* of the forms of national oppression, *consequently*, etc.

However, take Poland's *specific* conditions in place of these general arguments: her independence *today* is "impracticable" without wars or revolutions. To be in favour of an all-European war merely for the sake of restoring Poland is to be a nationalist of the worst sort, and to place the interests of a small number of Poles above those of the hundreds of millions of people who suffer from war. Such, indeed, are the "Fracy" (the Right wing of the P.S.P.[84]) who are socialists only in word, and compared with whom the Polish Social-Democrats are a thousand times right. To raise the question of Poland's independence *today*, with the *existing* alignment of the *neighbouring* imperialist powers, is really to run after a will-o'-the-wisp, plunge into narrow-minded nationalism and forget the necessary premise of an all-European or at least a Russian and a German revolution. To have put forward in 1908-14 freedom of coalition in Russia as an independent slogan would also have meant running after a will-o'-the-wisp, and would, objectively, have helped the Stolypin labour party (now the Potresov-Gvozdyov party, which, incidentally, is the same thing). But it would be madness to remove freedom of coalition in general from the programme of Social-Democracy!

A third and, perhaps, the most important example. We read in the Polish theses (III, end of § 2) that the idea of an independent Polish buffer state is opposed on the grounds that it is an "inane utopia of small impotent groups. Put into effect, it would mean the creation of a tiny fragment of a Polish state that would be a military colony of one or another group of Great Powers, a plaything of their military or economic interests, an area exploited by foreign capital, and a battlefield in future wars". This is all very *true* when used as an argument *against* the slogan of Polish independence *today*, because even a revolution in Poland alone would change nothing and would only divert the attention of the masses in Poland from *the main thing*—the connection between their struggle and that of the Russian and German proletariat. It is not a paradox but a fact that today the Polish proletariat as such can help the cause of socialism and freedom, *including the freedom of Poland*, only by *joint* struggle with the proletariat of the neighbouring countries, against the *narrow Polish* nationalists. The great historical service rendered by the Polish Social-Democrats in the struggle against the nationalists cannot possibly be denied.

But these same arguments, which are true from the standpoint of Poland's *specific* conditions in the *present* epoch, are manifestly untrue in the *general* form in which they are presented. So long as there are wars, Poland will always remain a battlefield in wars between Germany and Russia, but this is no argument against greater political liberty (and, therefore, against political independence) in the periods between wars. The same applies to the arguments about exploitation by foreign capital and Poland's role as a plaything of foreign interests. The Polish Social-Democrats cannot, at the moment, raise the slogan of Poland's independence, for the Poles, as proletarian internationalists, can do *nothing* about it without stooping, like the "Fracy", to humble servitude to *one* of the imperialist monarchies. But it is *not* indifferent to the Russian and German workers whether Poland is independent, or they take part in annexing her (and that would mean educating the Russian and German workers and peasants in the basest turpitude and their consent to play the part of executioner of other peoples).

The situation is, indeed, bewildering, but there is a way out in which *all* participants would remain internationalists: the Russian and German Social-Democrats by demanding for Poland unconditional *"freedom* to secede"; the Polish Social-Democrats by working for the unity of the proletarian struggle in both small and big countries without putting forward the slogan of Polish independence for the given epoch or the given period.

9. Engels's Letter to Kautsky

In his pamphlet *Socialism and Colonial Politics* (Berlin, 1907), Kautsky, who was then still a Marxist, published a letter written to him by Engels, dated September 12, 1882, which is extremely interesting in relation to the question under discussion. Here is the principal part of the letter.

"In my opinion the colonies proper, i.e., the countries occupied by a European population—Canada, the Cape, Australia—will all become independent; on the other hand, the countries inhabited by a native population, which are simply subjugated—India, Algeria, the Dutch, Portuguese and Spanish possessions—must be taken over for the time being by the proletariat and led as rapidly as possible towards independence. How this process will develop is difficult to say. India will perhaps, indeed very probably, make a revolution, and as a proletariat in process of self-emancipation cannot conduct any colonial wars, it would have to be allowed to run its course; it would not pass off without all sorts of destruction, of course, but that sort of thing is inseparable from all revolutions. The same might also take place elsewhere, e.g., in Algeria and Egypt, and would certainly be the best thing *for us*. We shall have enough to do at home. Once Europe is reorganised, and North America, that will furnish such colossal power and such an example that the semi-civilised countries will of themselves follow in their wake; economic needs, if anything, will see to that. But as to what social and political phases these countries will then have to pass through before they likewise arrive at socialist organisation, I think we today can advance only rather idle hypotheses. One thing alone is certain: *the victorious proletariat can force no blessings of any kind upon any foreign nation without undermining its own victory by so doing.* Which of course by no means excludes defensive wars of various kinds....".[85]

Engels does not at all suppose that the "economic" alone will directly remove all difficulties. An economic revolution will be a stimulus to *all* peoples to *strive* for socialism; but at the same time revolutions—against the socialist state—and wars are possible. Politics will inevitably adapt themselves to the economy, but not immediately or smoothly, not simply, not directly. Engels mentions as "certain" only one, absolutely internationalist, principle, and this he applies to *all* "foreign nations", i.e., not to colonial nations only: to force blessings upon them would mean to undermine the victory of the proletariat.

Just because the proletariat has carried out a social-revolution it will not become holy and immune from errors and weaknesses. But it will be inevitably led to realise this truth by possible errors (and selfish interest—attempts to saddle others).

We of the Zimmerwald Left all hold the same conviction as Kautsky, for example, held before his desertion of Marxism for the defence of chauvinism in 1914, namely, that the socialist revolution is quite possible *in the very near* future—"any day", as Kautsky himself once put it. National antipathies will not disappear so quickly: the hatred—and perfectly legitimate hatred—of an oppressed nation for its oppressor *will last* for a while; it will evaporate only *after* the victory of socialism and *after* the final establishment of completely democratic relations between nations. If we are to be faithful to socialism we must even now educate the masses in the spirit of internationalism, which is impossible in oppressor nations without advocating freedom of secession for oppressed nations.

10. The Irish Rebellion of 1916

Our theses were written before the outbreak of this rebellion, which must be the touchstone of our theoretical views.

The views of the opponents of self-determination lead to the conclusion that the vitality of small nations oppressed by imperialism has already been sapped, that they cannot play any role against imperialism, that support of their purely national aspirations will lead to nothing, etc. The imperialist war of 1914-16 has provided *facts* which refute such conclusions.

The war proved to be an epoch of crisis for the West-European nations, and for imperialism as a whole. Every crisis discards the conventionalities, tears away the outer wrappings, sweeps away the obsolete and reveals the underlying springs and forces. What has it revealed from the standpoint of the movement of oppressed nations? In the colonies there have been a number of attempts at rebellion, which the oppressor nations, naturally, did all they could to hide by means of a military censorship. Nevertheless, it is known that in Singapore the British brutally suppressed a mutiny among their Indian troops; that there were attempts at rebellion in French Annam (see *Nashe Slovo*[86]) and in the German Cameroons (see the Junius pamphlet); that in Europe, on the one hand, there was a rebellion in Ireland, which the "freedom-loving" English, who did not dare to extend conscription to Ireland, suppressed by executions, and, on the other, the Austrian Government passed the death sentence on the deputies of the Czech Diet "for treason", and shot whole Czech regiments for the same "crime".

This list is, of course, far from complete. Nevertheless, it proves that, *owing* to the crisis of imperialism, the flames of national revolt have flared up *both* in the colonies and in Europe, and that national sympathies and antipathies have manifested themselves in spite of the Draconian threats and measures of repression. All this before the crisis of imperialism hit its peak; the power of the imperialist bourgeoisie was yet to be undermined (this may be brought about by a war of "attrition" but has not yet happened) and the proletarian movements in the imperialist countries were still very feeble. What will happen when the war has caused complete exhaustion, or when, in one state at least, the power of the bourgeoisie has been shaken under the blows of proletarian struggle, as that of tsarism in 1905?

On May 9, 1916, there appeared in *Berner Tagwacht*, the organ of the Zimmerwald group, including some of the Leftists, an article on the Irish rebellion entitled "Their Song Is Over" and signed with the initials K. R.[87] It described the Irish rebellion as being nothing more nor less than a "putsch", for, as the author argued, "the Irish question was an agrarian one", the peasants had been pacified by reforms, and the nationalist movement remained only a "purely urban, petty-bourgeois movement, which, notwithstanding the sensation it caused, had not much social backing".

It is not surprising that this monstrously doctrinaire and pedantic assessment coincided with that of a Russian national-liberal Cadet, Mr. A. Kulisher (*Rech* No. 102, April 15, 1916), who also labelled the rebellion "the Dublin putsch".

It is to be hoped that, in accordance with the adage, "it's an ill wind that blows nobody any good", many comrades, who were not aware of the morass they were sinking into by repudiating "self-determination" and by treating the national movements of small nations with disdain, will have their eyes opened by the "accidental" coincidence of opinion held by a Social-Democrat and a representative of the imperialist bourgeoisie!!

The term "putsch", in its scientific sense, may be employed only when the attempt at insurrection has revealed nothing but a circle of conspirators or stupid maniacs, and has aroused no sympathy among the masses. The centuries-old Irish national movement, having passed through various stages and combinations of class interest, manifested itself, in particular, in a mass Irish National Congress in America (*Vorwärts*, March 20, 1916) which called for Irish independence; it also manifested itself in street fighting conducted by a section of the urban petty bourgeoisie *and a section of the workers* after a long period of mass agitation, demonstrations, suppression of newspapers, etc. Whoever calls *such* a rebellion a "putsch" is either a hardened reactionary, or a doctrinaire hopelessly incapable of envisaging a social revolution as a living phenomenon.

To imagine that social revolution is *conceivable* without revolts by small nations in the colonies and in Europe, without revolutionary outbursts by a section of the petty bourgeoisie *with all its prejudices*, without a movement of the politically non-conscious proletarian and semi-proletarian masses against oppression by the landowners, the church, and the monarchy, against national oppression, etc. —to imagine all this is to *repudiate social revolution*. So one army lines up in one place and says, "We are for socialism", and another, somewhere else and says, "We are for imperialism", and that will be a social revolution! Only those who hold such a ridiculously pedantic view could vilify the Irish rebellion by calling it a "putsch".

Whoever expects a "pure" social revolution will *never* live to see it. Such a person pays lip-service to revolution without understanding what revolution is.

The Russian Revolution of 1905 was a bourgeois-democratic revolution. It consisted of a series of battles in which *all* the discontented classes, groups and elements of the population participated. Among these there were masses imbued with the crudest prejudices, with the vaguest and most fantastic aims of struggle; there were small groups which accepted Japanese money, there were speculators and adventurers, etc. But *objectively*, the mass movement was breaking the back of tsarism and paving the way for democracy; for this reason the class-conscious workers led it.

The socialist revolution in Europe *cannot be* anything other than an outburst of mass struggle on the part of all and sundry oppressed and discontented elements. Inevitably, sections of the petty bourgeoisie and of the backward workers will participate in it—without such participation, *mass* struggle is *impossible*, without it *no* revolution is possible—and just as inevitably will they bring into the movement their prejudices, their reactionary fantasies, their weaknesses and errors. But *objectively* they will attack *capital*, and the class-conscious vanguard of the revolution, the advanced proletariat, expressing this objective truth of a variegated and discordant, motley and outwardly fragmented, mass struggle, will be able to unite and direct it, capture power, seize the banks, expropriate the trusts which all hate (though for different reasons!), and introduce other dictatorial measures which in their totality will amount to the overthrow of the bourgeoisie and the victory of socialism, which, however, will by no means immediately "purge" itself of petty-bourgeois slag.

Social-Democracy, we read in the Polish theses (I, 4), "must utilise the struggle of the young colonial bourgeoisie against European imperialism *in order to sharpen the revolutionary crisis in Europe*". (Authors' italics.)

Is it not clear that it is least of all permissible to contrast Europe to the colonies in *this* respect? The struggle of the oppressed nations *in Europe*, a struggle capable of going all the way to insurrection and street fighting, capable of breaking down the iron discipline of the army and martial law, will "sharpen the revolutionary crisis in Europe" to an infinitely greater degree than a much more developed rebellion in a remote colony. A blow delivered against the power of the English imperialist bourgeoisie by a rebellion in Ireland is a hundred times more significant politically than a blow of equal force delivered in Asia or in Africa.

The French chauvinist press recently reported the publication in Belgium of the eightieth issue of an illegal journal, *Free Belgium*. Of course, the chauvinist press of France very often lies, but this piece of news seems to be true. Whereas chauvinist and Kautskyite German Social-Democracy has failed to establish a free press for itself during the two years of war, and has meekly borne the yoke of military censorship (only the Left Radical elements, to their credit be it said, have published pamphlets and manifestos, in spite of the censorship)—an oppressed civilised nation has reacted to a military oppression unparalleled in ferocity by establishing an organ of revolutionary protest!

The dialectics of history are such that small nations, power-less as an *independent* factor in the struggle against imperialism, play a part as one of the ferments, one of the bacilli, which help the *real* anti-imperialist force, the socialist proletariat, to make its appearance on the scene.

The general staffs in the current war are doing their utmost to utilise any national and revolutionary movement in the enemy camp: the Germans utilise the Irish rebellion, the French—the Czech movement, etc. They are acting quite correctly from their own point of view. A serious war would not be treated seriously if advantage were not taken of the enemy's slightest weakness and if every opportunity that presented itself were not seized upon, the more so since it is impossible to know beforehand at what moment, where, and with what force some powder magazine will "explode". We would be very poor revolutionaries if, in the proletariat's great war of liberation for socialism, we did not know how to utilise *every* popular movement against *every single* disaster imperialism brings in order to intensify and extend the crisis. If we were, on the one hand, to repeat in a thousand keys the declaration that we are "opposed" to all national oppression and, on the other, to describe the heroic revolt of the most mobile and enlightened section of certain classes in an oppressed nation against its oppressors as a "putsch", we should be sinking to the same level of stupidity as the Kautskyites.

It is the misfortune of the Irish that they rose prematurely, before the European revolt of the proletariat had *had time* to mature. Capitalism is not so harmoniously built that the various sources of rebellion can immediately merge of their own accord, without reverses and defeats. On the other hand, the very fact that revolts do break out at different times, in different places, and are of different kinds, guarantees wide scope and depth to the general movement; but it is only in premature, individual, sporadic and therefore unsuccessful, revolutionary movements that the masses gain experience, acquire knowledge, gather strength, and get to know their real leaders, the socialist proletarians, and in this way prepare for the general onslaught, just as certain strikes, demonstrations, local and national, mutinies in the army, outbreaks among the peasantry, etc., prepared the way for the general onslaught in 1905.

11. Conclusion

Contrary to the erroneous assertions of the Polish Social-Democrats, the demand for the self-determination of nations has played no less a role in our Party agitation than, for example, the arming of the people, the separation of the church from the state, the election of civil servants by the people and other points the philistines have called "utopian". On the contrary, the strengthening of the national movements after 1905 naturally prompted more vigorous agitation by our Party, including a number of articles in 1912-13, and the resolution of our Party in 1913 giving a precise "anti-Kautskian" definition (i.e., one that does not tolerate purely verbal "recognition") of the *content* of the point.*

It will not do to overlook a fact which was revealed at that early date: opportunists of various nationalities, the Ukrainian Yurkevich, the Bundist Liebman, Semkovsky, the Russian myrmidon of Potresov and Co., all spoke *in favour* of Rosa Luxemburg's arguments *against* self-determination! What for Rosa Luxemburg, the Polish Social-Democrat, had been merely an incorrect theoretical generalisation of the *specific* conditions of the movement in Poland, became *objective* opportunist support for Great-Russian imperialism when actually applied to more extensive circumstances, to conditions obtaining in a big state instead of a small one, when applied on an international scale instead of the narrow Polish scale. The history of *trends* in political thought (as distinct from the views of individuals) has proved the correctness of our programme.

Outspoken social-imperialists, such as Lensch, still rail both against self-determination and the renunciation of annexations. As for the Kautskyites, they hypocritically recognise self-determination—Trotsky and Martov are going the same way here in Russia. *Both of them*, like Kautsky, say they favour self-determination. What happens in practice? Take Trotsky's articles "The Nation and the Economy" in *Nashe Slovo*, and you will find his usual eclecticism: on the one hand, the economy unites nations and, on the other, national oppression divides them. The

---

* See V. I. Lenin, *Collected Works*, Vol. 19, pp. 427-29.—*Ed.*

conclusion? The conclusion is that the prevailing hypocrisy remains unexposed, agitation is dull and does not touch upon what is most important, basic, significant and closely connected with practice—one's attitude to the nation that is oppressed by "one's own" nation. Martov and other secretaries abroad simply preferred to forget—a profitable lapse of memory!—the struggle of their colleague and fellow-member Semkovsky against self-determination. In the legal press of the Gvozdyovites[88] (*Nash Golos*) Martov spoke *in favour* of self-determination, pointing out the indisputable truth that during the imperialist war it does not *yet* imply participation, etc., but evading the main thing—he also evades it in the illegal, free press!—which is that *even in peace time* Russia set a world record for the oppression of nations with an imperialism that is much more crude, medieval, economically backward and militarily bureaucratic. The Russian Social-Democrat who "recognises" the self-determination of nations more or less as it is recognised by Messrs. Plekhanov, Potresov and Co., that is, without bothering to fight for the freedom of secession for nations oppressed by tsarism, is *in fact* an imperialist and a lackey of tsarism.

No matter what the subjective "good" intentions of Trotsky and Martov may be, their evasiveness objectively supports Russian social-imperialism. The epoch of imperialism has turned all the "great" powers into the oppressors of a number of nations, and the development of imperialism will inevitably lead to a more definite division of trends in this question in international Social-Democracy as well.

Written in July 1916

Published in October 1916
in *Sbornik Sotsial-Demokrata* No. 1
Signed: *N. Lenin*

Collected Works, Vol. 22

THE QUESTION OF NATIONALITIES
OR "AUTONOMISATION"[89]

I suppose I have been very remiss with respect to the workers of Russia for not having intervened energetically and decisively enough in the notorious question of autonom·isation, which, it appears, is officially called the question of the union of Soviet socialist republics.

When this question arose last summer, I was ill; and then in autumn I relied too much on my recovery and on the October and December plenary meetings[90] giving me an opportunity of intervening in this question. However, I did not manage to attend the October Plenary Meeting (when this question came up) or the one in December, and so the question passed me by almost completely.

I have only had time for a talk with Comrade Dzerzhinsky, who came from the Caucasus and told me how this matter stood in Georgia. I have also managed to exchange a few words with Comrade Zinoviev and express my apprehensions on this matter. From what I was told by Comrade Dzerzhinsky, who was at the head of the commission sent by the C.C. to "investigate" the Georgian incident, I could only draw the greatest apprehensions. If matters had come to such a pass that Orjonikidze could go to the extreme of applying physical violence, as Comrade Dzerzhinsky informed me, we can imagine what a mess we have got ourselves into. Obviously the whole business of "autonomisation" was radically wrong and badly timed.

It is said that a united apparatus was needed. But where did that assurance come from? Did it not come from that same Russian apparatus which, as I pointed out in one of the preceding sections of my diary, we took over from tsarism and slightly anointed with Soviet oil?

There is no doubt that that measure should have been delayed somewhat until we could say that we vouched for our apparatus as our own. But now, we must, in all conscience, admit the contrary; the apparatus we call ours is, in fact, still quite alien to us; it is a bourgeois and tsarist hotch-potch and there has been no possibility of getting rid of it in the course of the past five years without the help of other countries and because we have been "busy" most of the time with military engagements and the fight against famine.

It is quite natural that in such circumstances the "freedom to secede from the union" by which we justify ourselves will be a mere scrap of paper, unable to defend the non-Russians from the onslaught of that really Russian man, the Great-Russian chauvinist, in substance a rascal and a tyrant, such as the typical Russian bureaucrat is. There is no doubt that the infinitesimal percentage of Soviet and sovietised workers will drown in that tide of chauvinistic Great-Russian riffraff like a fly in milk.

It is said in defence of this measure that the People's Commissariats directly concerned with national psychology and national education were set up as separate bodies. But there the question arises: can these People's Commissariats be made quite independent? and secondly: were we careful enough to take measures to provide the non-Russians with a real safeguard against the truly Russian bully? I do not think we took such measures although we could and should have done so.

I think that Stalin's haste and his infatuation with pure administration, together with his spite against the notorious "nationalist-socialism", played a fatal role here. In politics spite generally plays the basest of roles.

I also fear that Comrade Dzerzhinsky, who went to the Caucasus to investigate the "crime" of those "nationalist-socialists", distinguished himself there by his truly Russian frame of mind (it is common knowledge that people of other nationalities who have become Russified overdo this Russian frame of mind) and that the impartiality of his whole commission was typified well enough by Orjonikidze's "manhandling". I think that no provocation or even insult can justify such Russian manhandling and that Comrade Dzerzhinsky was inexcusably guilty in adopting a light-hearted attitude towards it.

For all the citizens in the Caucasus Orjonikidze was the authority. Orjonikidze had no right to display that irritability to which he and Dzerzhinsky referred. On the contrary, Orjonikidze should have behaved with a restraint which cannot be demanded of any ordinary citizen, still less of a man accused of a "political" crime. And, to tell the truth, those nationalist-socialists were citizens who were accused of a political crime, and the terms of the accusation were such that it could not be described otherwise.

Here we have an important question of principle: how is internationalism to be understood?*

Lenin

December 30, 1922
Taken down by M. V.

---

* After this the following phrase was crossed out in the shorthand text: "It seems to me that our comrades have not studied this important question of principle sufficiently."—*Ed.*

Continuation of the notes.
December 31, 1922.

THE QUESTION OF NATIONALITIES
OR "AUTONOMISATION"
(Continued)

In my writings on the national question I have already said that an abstract presentation of the question of nationalism in general is of no use at all. A distinction must necessarily be made between the nationalism of an oppressor nation and that of an oppressed nation, the nationalism of a big nation and that of a small nation.

In respect of the second kind of nationalism we, nationals of a big nation, have nearly always been guilty, in historic practice, of an infinite number of cases of violence; furthermore, we commit violence and insult an infinite number of times without noticing it. It is sufficient to recall my Volga reminiscences of how non-Russians are treated; how the Poles are not called by any other name than Polyachishka, how the Tatar is nicknamed Prince, how the Ukrainians are always Khokhols and the Georgians and other Caucasian nationals always Kapkasians.

That is why internationalism on the part of oppressors or "great" nations, as they are called (though they are great only in their violence, only great as bullies), must consist not only in the observance of the formal equality of nations but even in an inequality of the oppressor nation, the great nation, that must make up for the inequality which obtains in actual practice. Anybody who does not understand this has not grasped the real proletarian attitude to the national question, he is still essentially petty bourgeois in his point of view and is, therefore, sure to descend to the bourgeois point of view.

What is important for the proletarian? For the proletarian it is not only important, it is absolutely essential that he should be assured that the non-Russians place the greatest possible trust in the proletarian class struggle. What is needed to ensure this? Not merely formal equality. In one way or another, by one's attitude or by concessions, it is necessary to compensate the non-Russians for the lack of trust, for the suspicion and the insults to which the government of the "dominant" nation subjected them in the past.

I think it is unnecessary to explain this to Bolsheviks, to Communists, in greater detail. And I think that in the present instance, as far as the Georgian nation is concerned, we have a typical case in which a genuinely proletarian attitude makes profound caution, thoughtfulness and a readiness to compromise a matter of necessity for us. The Georgian who is neglectful of this aspect of the question, or who carelessly flings about accusations of "nationalist-socialism" (whereas he himself is a real and true "nationalist-socialist", and even a vulgar Great-Russian bully), violates, in substance, the interests of proletarian class solidarity, for nothing holds up the development and strengthening of proletarian class solidarity so much as national injustice; "offended" nationals are not sensitive to anything so much as to the feeling of equality and the violation of this equality, if only through negligence or jest—to the violation of that equality by their proletarian comrades. That is why in this case it is better to overdo rather than underdo the concessions and leniency towards the national minorities. That is why, in this case, the fundamental interest of proletarian solidarity, and consequently of the proletarian class struggle, requires that we never adopt a formal attitude to the national question, but always take into account the specific attitude of the proletarian of the oppressed (or small) nation towards the oppressor (or great) nation.

Lenin

Taken down by M. V.
December 31, 1922.

———

Continuation of the notes.
December 31, 1922.

What practical measures must be taken in the present situation?

Firstly, we must maintain and strengthen the union of socialist republics. Of this there can be no doubt. This measure is necessary for us and it is necessary for the world communist proletariat in its struggle against the world bourgeoisie and its defence against bourgeois intrigues.

Secondly, the union of socialist republics must be retained for its diplomatic apparatus. By the way, this apparatus is an exceptional component of our state apparatus. We have not allowed a single influential person from the old tsarist apparatus into it. All sections with any authority are composed of Communists. That is why it has already won for itself (this may be said boldly) the name of a reliable communist apparatus purged to an incomparably greater extent of the old tsarist, bourgeois and petty-bourgeois elements than that which we have had to make do with in other People's Commissariats.

Thirdly, exemplary punishment must be inflicted on Comrade Orjonikidze (I say this all the more regretfully as I am one of his personal friends and have worked with him abroad) and the investigation of all the material which Dzerzhinsky's commission has collected must be completed or started over again to correct the enormous mass of wrongs and biased judgements which it doubtlessly contains. The political responsibility for all this truly Great-Russian nationalist campaign must, of course, be laid on Stalin and Dzerzhinsky.

Fourthly, the strictest rules must be introduced on the use of the national language in the non-Russian republics of our union, and these rules must be checked with special care. There is no doubt that our apparatus being what it is, there is bound to be, on the pretext of unity in the railway service, unity in the fiscal service and so on, a mass of truly Russian abuses. Special ingenuity is necessary for the struggle against these abuses, not to mention special sincerity on the part of those who undertake this struggle. A detailed code will be required, and only the nationals living in the republic in question can draw it up at all successfully. And then we cannot be sure in advance that as a result of this work we shall not take a step backward at our next Congress of Soviets, i.e., retain the union of Soviet socialist republics only for military and diplomatic affairs, and in all other respects restore full independence to the individual People's Commissariats.

It must be borne in mind that the decentralisation of the People's Commissariats and the lack of co-ordination in their work as far as Moscow and other centres are concerned can be compensated sufficiently by Party authority, if it is exercised with sufficient prudence and impartiality; the harm that can result to our state from a lack of unification between the national apparatuses and the Russian apparatus is infinitely less than that which will be done not only to us, but to the whole International, and to the hundreds of millions of the peoples of Asia, which is destined to follow us on to the stage of history in the near future. It would be unpardonable opportunism if, on the eve of the debut of the East, just as it is awakening, we undermined our prestige with its peoples, even if only by the slightest crudity or injustice towards our own non-Russian nationalities. The need to rally against the imperialists of the West, who are defending the capitalist world, is one thing. There can be no doubt about that and it would be superfluous for me to speak about my unconditional approval of it. It is another thing when we ourselves lapse, even if only in trifles, into imperialist attitudes towards oppressed nationalities, thus undermining all our principled sincerity, all our principled defence of the struggle against imperialism. But the morrow of world history will be a day when the awakening peoples oppressed by imperialism are finally aroused and the decisive long and hard struggle for their liberation begins.

Lenin

December 31, 1922
Taken down by M. V.

NOTES

[1] *Notification (Izveshcheniye)*—the abridged title of the pamphlet *Notification and Resolutions of the 1913 Summer Conference of the Central Committee of the Russian Social-Democratic Labour Party and Leading Party Workers*, published by the Central Committee in 1913.   p. 5

[2] The article referred to is J. V. Stalin's "Marxism and the National Question" written at the end of 1912 and the beginning of 1913 in Vienna and published in the magazine *Prosveshcheniye* (Enlightenment), Nos. 3, 4, 5 for 1913 under the title "The National Question and Social-Democracy".   p. 5

[3] *Stolypin P. A.* (1862-1911)—Chairman of the Russian Council of Ministers from July 1906; a reactionary. His name is associated with a period in Russian history known as the "Stolypin reaction" during which military tribunals passed savage sentences and the death penalty was widely applied.
     Maklakov N. A. (1871-1918)—Minister for Internal Affairs from December 1913 to June 1915, Chief of the Gendarmerie and Member of the State Council from 1915 (extreme Right wing); a reactionary.
                                                                            p. 5

[4] *Economism*—an opportunist trend in Russian Social-Democracy at the turn of the twentieth century; a Russian variant of international opportunism. In his *What Is To be Done?* Lenin subjected Economism to a devastating criticism.   p. 6

[5] *"Legal Marxism"*—a trend in Russian Social-Democracy. Its representatives, the "legal Marxists", were bourgeois intellectuals who expounded their views in legal newspapers and magazines—i.e., those permitted by the tsarist censorship—under the flag of Marxism. They attempted to adapt Marxism and the working-class movement to the needs of the bourgeoisie.   p. 6

[6] *Menshevism*—a petty-bourgeois opportunist trend in Russian Social-Democracy which brought a bourgeois influence to bear on the working class. The Mensheviks got their name at the Second Congress of the R.S.D.L.P. in August 1903; in the elections to the

Party's leading bodies held at the end of the Congress they were in the minority (*menshinstvo*) and the revolutionary Social-Democrats, headed by Lenin, were in the majority (*bolshinstvo*), hence, the names Mensheviks and Bolsheviks. The Mensheviks strove to obtain an agreement between the proletariat and the bourgeoisie and pursued an opportunist line in the working-class movement. After the February bourgeois-democratic revolution in 1917 dual power was set up in Russia: the dictatorship of the bourgeoisie—the bourgeois Provisional Government, and that of the proletariat and peasantry—the Soviets. The Mensheviks and the Socialist-Revolutionaries took part in the Provisional Government, supported its imperialist policy and fought against the growing proletarian revolution. The Mensheviks pursued the same policy—that of supporting the Provisional Government and diverting the masses from the revolutionary movement—in the Soviets as well.

After the October Revolution the Mensheviks became an open counter-revolutionary party, they organised and participated in conspiracies and revolts aimed at the overthrow of Soviet power.

p. 6

[7] *Liquidationism*—an opportunist line pursued by the Menshevik Social-Democrats after the defeat of the 1905-07 Revolution in Russia.

The liquidators demanded the liquidation of the illegal revolutionary party of the working class. They called on the workers to cease their revolutionary struggle against tsarism and intended to call a non-party "workers' congress" at which an opportunist "broad working-class party" was to be set up, a party that would renounce revolutionary slogans and engage solely in legal activity permitted by the tsarist government. Lenin and other Bolsheviks persistently exposed the liquidators as traitors to the revolution. The liquidators met with no success among the working-class masses. The Prague Conference of the R.S.D.L.P., held in January 1912, expelled them from the Party.

p. 6

[8] *Iskra* (The Spark)—the first illegal all-Russia Marxist political newspaper, founded by Lenin in 1900. The first issue of Lenin's *Iskra* was published in Leipzig and subsequent issues appeared in Munich; from April 1902, the paper was published in London and from the spring of 1903, in Geneva. *Iskra* served to consolidate the Party ideologically and organisationally. On Lenin's initiative and with his direct participation, the *Iskra* editorial board drew up a draft programme for the Party and prepared the Second Congress of the R.S.D.L.P. that was held in July and August 1903. Lenin and his supporters used the columns of *Iskra* for the revolutionary Marxist struggle against the Economists, against all manifestations of opportunism in the international working-class movement, and against the revisionists in Russian and West-European Social-Democracy. A special decision adopted by the Second Congress of the R.S.D.L.P. noted the exceptional role played by *Iskra* in the struggle for the Party and declared it the central organ of the R.S.D.L.P. After the Second Congress the Mensheviks,

aided by Plekhanov, seized *Iskra* and beginning with issue No. 52, converted it into the organ of their own faction. From that moment it became customary to speak of the *New Iskra*, the Menshevik opportunist paper, to distinguish it from the *old Leninist*, Bolshevik *Iskra*.   p. 6

[9] *Bund*—the Jewish General Labour League in Lithuania, Poland and Russia, which was organised in 1897 and was mainly an association of Jewish artisans living in the western regions of Russia. The Bund was affiliated to the R.S.D.L.P. at its First Congress in March 1898. At the Second Congress of the R.S.D.L.P. held between July 17 (30) and August 10 (23), 1903 the Bund representatives demanded that the Bund be recognised as the sole representative of the Jewish proletariat; the Congress rejected this organisational nationalism of the Bund and the latter left the Party.

After the Fourth (Unity) Congress in 1906 the Bund again entered the R.S.D.L.P. Its members gave constant support to the Mensheviks and fought against the Bolsheviks. Although it belonged, formally, to the R.S.D.L.P., the Bund was a bourgeois nationalist organisation. It put forward the demand for cultural-national autonomy in opposition to the Bolshevik programme demand for the right of nations to self-determination. The Bund played an active part in the foundation of the August anti-Party bloc. At the Prague Conference of the R.S.D.L.P., in January 1912, its members were expelled from the Party together with other opportunists. During the First World War the Bund members adopted the position of social-chauvinism; in 1917 the Bund supported the Provisional Government and fought on the side of the enemies of the October Socialist Revolution. During the Civil War leading Bundists joined ranks with the counter-revolutionary forces. At the same time there was a change taking place among rank-and-file members of the Bund who began to favour collaboration with Soviet power. When the victory of the proletarian dictatorship over the internal counter-revolution and foreign intervention became obvious the Bund declared that they would renounce their struggle against Soviet power. In March 1921 the Bund announced its dissolution and part of its membership entered the Russian Communist Party (Bolsheviks).   p. 6

[10] *Zarya* (Dawn)—a Marxist scientific and political magazine; in 1901 and 1902 it was published in Stuttgart by the *Iskra* editorial board. Altogether four numbers were published in three issues: No. 1—April 1901 (it actually appeared on March 23, N.S.), No. 2-3—December 1901 and No. 4—August 1902.   p. 10

[11] The article "Critical Remarks on the National Question" was written between October and December 1913 and printed that same year in the Bolshevik legal magazine *Prosveshcheniye* Nos. 10, 11 and 12.

The article was preceded by a number of lectures on the national question given by Lenin in the summer of 1913 in several Swiss towns—Zurich, Geneva, Lausanne and Berne.

In the autumn of 1913 Lenin made a report on the national question to the August (Summer) Conference of the Central Committee of the R.S.D.L.P. and leading Party workers. A resolution written by Lenin was passed on the basis of his report. After the Conference Lenin began work on the article.　　　　p. 12

[12] *Severnaya Pravda* (Northern Truth)—one of the names of the Bolshevik daily legal newspaper *Pravda*; the paper was published under this name from August 1 to September 7, 1913.　　p. 12

[13] *Zeit* (Time)—a weekly newspaper, the organ of the Bund; it was published in St. Petersburg from December 1912 to June 1914.

p. 12

[14] *Dzvin* (The Bell)—a legal monthly nationalist magazine, Menshevist in trend; it was published in Ukrainian in Kiev from January 1913 to the middle of 1914.　　　　p. 12

[15] *Black Hundreds*—monarchist gangs formed by the tsarist police for the struggle against the revolutionary movement. The Black Hundreds assassinated revolutionaries, attacked the progressive intelligentsia and organised Jewish pogroms.　　　　p. 13

[16] *Russkoye Slovo* (Russian Word)—a bourgeois liberal daily published in Moscow from 1895; it was closed down in November 1917.　p. 13

[17] *Pale of Settlement*—territories in tsarist Russia outside of which Jews were not permitted to live.　　　　p. 22

[18] In tsarist Russia only a limited percentage of Jews was accepted into state service, and the middle and higher schools belonging to the state.　　　　p. 22

[19] *J.S.L.P.* (Jewish Socialist Labour Party)—a petty-bourgeois nationalist organisation founded in 1906. The basis of the J.S.L.P. programme was national autonomy for the Jews—the formation of extra-territorial Jewish parliaments (diets) empowered to decide questions concerning the political organisation of Jews in Russia. The J.S.L.P. was close to the Socialist-Revolutionaries in politics and joined them in the struggle against the R.S.D.L.P.　　　p. 29

[20] *Beilis case*—a court case staged by the tsarist government in Kiev in 1913. A Jew named Beilis was falsely accused of the murder of a Christian boy, Yushchinsky, for ritual purposes (the murder was actually committed by members of the Black Hundreds). The tsarist government, in staging this trial, tried to fan the flames of anti-Semitism and start Jewish pogroms for the purpose of diverting the attention of the masses from the revolutionary movement that was growing strong in the country. The trial aroused great indignation among the public; in a number of towns there were workers' demonstrations of protest. Beilis was acquitted by the court. p. 30

²¹ *Socialist-Revolutionaries* (S.R.s)—a petty-bourgeois party that
emerged in Russia in 1901-02 as a result of the amalgamation of
a number of Narodnik groups and circles (the Union of Socialist-
Revolutionaries, the Party of Socialist-Revolutionaries and others).
Its official organs were the newspaper *Revolutsionnaya Rossiya*
(Revolutionary Russia) (1900-05) and the magazine *Vestnik Rus-
skoi Revolutsii* (Herald of the Russian Revolution) (1901-05). The
political views of the S.R.s were an eclectic mixture of the ideas
of the Narodniks and of revisionism; they tried, to use Lenin's
expression, to "patch up the rents in the Narodnik ideas with
bits of fashionable opportunist 'criticism' of Marxism" (V. I. Lenin,
Collected Works, Vol. 9, p. 310). The S.R.s did not see any class
differences between the proletariat and the peasantry, they ignored
the class stratification and contradictions within the peasantry and
denied the leading role of the proletariat in the revolution. The
tactics of individual terror which the S.R.s preached as the basic
method of fighting against the autocracy did great harm to the
revolutionary movement and impeded the organisation of the
masses for the revolutionary struggle.

The S.R. agrarian programme envisaged the abolition of private
land tenure and the transfer of the land to the village commune
for use on an equalitarian basis and also the development of every
type of co-operative organisation. This programme, which the
S.R.s tried to depict as a programme for "the socialisation of the
land", contained nothing socialist since the abolition of the private
ownership of land alone could not, as Lenin pointed out, abolish
the rule of capital and the poverty of the masses. The historically
progressive feature of the S.R. agrarian programme was the struggle
to abolish landed estates, a demand that objectively expressed the
interests and aspirations of the peasantry at the bourgeois-democratic stage of the revolution.

The Bolshevik Party exposed the S.R. attempt to masquerade
as socialists and carried on a stubborn struggle against the S.R.s
for influence among the peasantry; they also exposed the danger
which the S.R. tactics of individual terror constituted for the
working-class movement. At the same time Bolsheviks agreed, on
certain terms, to co-operate with the S.R.s in the struggle against
tsarism.

The class differentiation of the peasantry, in the final analysis,
was the cause of the political and ideological instability and the
organisational chaos in the S.R. Party, and their perpetual wavering between the liberal bourgeoisie and the proletariat. At the time
of the First Russian Revolution the S.R.s split into a Right wing,
which formed the legal Labour Popular Socialist Party close to
the Cadets in its views, and a Left wing that formed itself into a
semi-anarchist League of Maximalists. In the period known as the
Stolypin reaction the Socialist-Revolutionary Party suffered a
complete ideological and organisational collapse. During the First
World War the majority of the S.R.s adopted the position of social-
chauvinism.

After the victory of the February revolution in 1917, the S.R.s,
together with the Mensheviks and Cadets, became the mainstay of

the bourgeois-landlord Provisional Government and the leaders of the party (Kerensky, Avksentyev, Chernov) were members of the Government. At the end of November 1917, as the peasantry grew more revolutionary, the "Left" S.R.s formed into a separate party. In an effort to retain their influence among the masses of the peasantry the "Left" S.R.s formally recognised Soviet power, and entered into an agreement with the Bolsheviks, but soon reverted to the struggle against Soviet power.

In the years of foreign intervention and Civil War the S.R.s conducted subversive counter-revolutionary activity, gave active support to the interventionists and whiteguard generals, took part in counter-revolutionary conspiracies, and organised terrorist acts against leaders of the Soviet state and the Communist Party. After the Civil War the S.R.s continued their hostile activities against the Soviet state both inside the country and in the camp of the whiteguards in emigration.   p. 31

[22] *P.S.P. (Polska partia socjalistyczna*—Polish Socialist Party)—a petty-bourgeois nationalist party founded in 1892. The P.S.P. based its programme on the struggle for the national liberation of Poland, conducted separatist, nationalist propaganda among the Polish workers and tried to divert their attention from the joint struggle together with the Russian workers against the autocracy and capitalism. In 1906 the P.S.P. split into the P.S.P. Left and a chauvinist Right wing, known as the "Revolutionary Faction of the P.S.P.", "Fracy".

Under the influence of the R.S.D.L.P.(B.) and of the Polish Social-Democratic Party and rank-and-file worker-members of the P.S.P. Left, the latter gradually got rid of its nationalism. During the First World War part of the P.S.P. Left adopted an internationalist position and in December 1918 united with the Polish Social-Democratic Party to form the Communist Workers' Party of Poland (a name which the Communist Party of Poland retained until 1925).

The P.S.P. Right continued its national-chauvinist policy during the First World War: it organised the Polish Legions that fought on the side of Austro-German imperialism.

On the formation of the Polish bourgeois state the Right wing retained the name P.S.P. When the party headed the government it handed over power to the bourgeoisie and conducted systematic anti-Soviet and anti-communist agitation, supporting the policy of aggression against the Soviet Union and the annexation and colonial oppression of the Western Ukraine and Western Byelorussia. After Pilsudski's fascist putsch (May 1926) the P.S.P. was formally in opposition but in actual fact collaborated with the fascists and continued its anti-Soviet propaganda.

During the Second World War the P.S.P. split for a second time. Its reactionary, chauvinist section, which adopted the name of W.R.N. (wolność, równość, niepodległość—liberty, equality, independence), collaborated with the fascists and took part in the reactionary Polish "government" in exile with its headquarters in London. The other section, the Left wing, calling itself the Workers'

Party of Polish Socialists (W.P.P.S.), under the influence of the Polish Workers' Party, founded in 1942, joined in a united front of struggle against the nazi occupants, fought for the liberation of Poland from fascist slavery and adopted a position favouring the establishment of friendly relations with the U.S.S.R.

In 1944, when the eastern part of Poland had been liberated from German occupation and the Polish Committee of National Liberation set up, the W.P.P.S. again took the name of P.S.P. and jointly with the Polish Workers' Party set about organising People's Democratic Poland. In December 1948 the Polish Socialist Party and the Polish Workers' Party united to form the Polish United Workers' Party.　　　　　　　　　　　　　　　　　　　　　　　　　p. 31

[23] *Luch* (The Ray)—a legal daily newspaper published by the Menshevik liquidators in St. Petersburg from September 1912 to July 1913; it was maintained by "the money *of rich friends from among the bourgeoisie*" (Lenin). From July 1913 *Luch* was replaced by the newspaper *Zhivaya Zhizn* (Real Life) and later by *Novaya Rabochaya Gazeta* (New Workers' Newspaper).　　　　　　　　　p. 31

[24] *Prosveshcheniye* (Enlightenment)—a Bolshevik theoretical magazine published legally in St. Petersburg from December 1911 to July 1914. On the eve of the First World War it was closed down by order of the government. The publication of *Prosveshcheniye* was resumed in the autumn of 1917, but only one issue, a double number, appeared.　　　　　　　　　　　　　　　　　　　　　p. 31

[25] *Bernsteinism*—a trend in international Social-Democracy, hostile to Marxism, that emerged in Germany at the end of the nineteenth century and got its name from Eduard Bernstein, a German Social-Democrat opportunist. After the death of Engels, Bernstein came out openly in favour of a revision of Marx's revolutionary theory in the spirit of bourgeois liberalism (in his articles "Problems of Socialism" and his book *The Premises of Socialism and the Tasks of Social-Democracy*), in an attempt to turn the Social-Democratic Party into a party of social reforms.

Supporters of Bernstein in Russia were the "legal Marxists", Economists, Bund members and the Mensheviks.　　　　　　p. 31

[26] *Novaya Rabochaya Gazeta* (New Workers' Newspaper)—a legal daily newspaper published by the Menshevik liquidators in St. Petersburg from August 1913. From January 30 (February 12), 1914, it was replaced by *Severnaya Rabochaya Gazeta* (Northern Workers' Newspaper) and then by *Nasha Rabochaya Gazeta* (Our Workers' Newspaper). Lenin frequently referred to this paper as the *New Liquidators' Paper*.　　　　　　　　　　　　　　　　　　　　p. 33

[27] Lenin's data are taken from the statistical handbook *One-Day Census of Elementary Schools in the Empire, made on January 18, 1911, Issue 1, Part 2. St. Petersburg Educational Area. Gubernias of Archangel, Vologda, Novgorod, Olonets, Pskov and St. Petersburg.* St. Petersburg, 1912, p. 72.　　　　　　　　　　　　　　p. 36

[28] *Dragomanov M. P.* (1841-1895)—Ukrainian historian and journalist; he expressed the ideology of Ukrainian bourgeois national-liberalism. p. 39

[29] *Przeglad Socjaldemokratyczny* (Social-Democratic Review)—a magazine published from 1902 to 1904 and from 1908 to 1910 in Cracow by Polish Social-Democrats, with Rosa Luxemburg's close collaboration. p. 39

[30] *Vestnik Yevropy* (European Messenger)—a magazine published monthly in St. Petersburg from 1866 to the spring of 1918. The magazine was the mouthpiece of the Russian liberal bourgeoisie; from the beginning of the nineties it conducted a systematic campaign against Marxism. p. 42

[31] *The 1903 Programme*—the programme of the Russian Social-Democratic Labour Party adopted at the Second Congress of the Party in 1903. p. 46

[32] *Die Neue Zeit* (New Times)—a German Social-Democratic journal published in Stuttgart from 1883 to 1923. A number of Frederick Engels's articles were published in it between 1885 and 1895. Engels gave frequent advice to its editors and sharply criticised them for deviations from Marxism. In the late nineties, after Engels's death, the magazine began the regular publication of revisionist articles. During the world imperialist war (1914-18) the magazine adopted a Centrist, Kautskyite position and supported the social-chauvinists. p. 47

[33] See K. Marx, *Capital*, Vol. I, Moscow 1965, p. 765. p. 49

[34] *Russkaya Mysl* (Russian Thought)—a liberal bourgeois monthly published in Moscow from 1880. After the 1905 revolution it became the organ of the Right wing of the Cadet Party. In this period of its existence Lenin called it "*Black-Hundred*" *Thought*. The magazine was closed down in the middle of 1918. p. 55

[35] *L. Vl.*—L. Vladimirov, pseudonym of M. K. Sheinfinkel. p. 63

[36] *June Third*—the coup d'état of June 3 (16), 1907 by which the government disbanded the Second Duma and amended the law on elections to the Duma. The new electoral law greatly increased the representation of landed proprietors, merchants and industrialists and greatly reduced the number of peasant and worker representatives that was already very small. The law deprived the greater part of the inhabitants of Asiatic Russia of their franchise and reduced the representation of Poland and the Caucasus to one half. The Third Duma that was elected under this law and which first met in November 1907 was, in composition, a Black-Hundred-Cadet Duma.

The June Third coup d'état marked the beginning of the period of the Stolypin reaction which was also known as the "June Third regime". p. 66

[37] *Octobrists,* or *The Union of October Seventeenth*—a counter-revolutionary party of the big merchant and industrial bourgeoisie and big landed proprietors who ran their estates on capitalist lines. It was formed in November 1905. In words the Octobrists recognised the manifesto of October 17 but in deed they unconditionally supported the home and foreign policy of the tsarist government. The leaders of the Octobrists were the big industrialist A. Guchkov and the owner of huge landed estates M. Rodzyanko.   p. 66

[38] *Progressists*—a party of the national-liberal monarchist bourgeoisie that took shape in the period of reaction. The Progressists championed "a moderate constitution with narrowly-restricted rights based on a bicameral system and an anti-democratic suffrage", they championed " 'a strong authority' that would pursue the 'patriotic' policy of conquering with sword and fire new markets for 'national industry' " (see V. I. Lenin, *Collected Works*, Vol. 18, p. 441).

Cadets—members of the Constitutional-Democratic Party, the leading party of the liberal monarchist bourgeoisie in Russia, formed in October 1905. The membership included liberal capitalists, landowners and bourgeois intellectuals. Subsequently, the Cadets became a party of the imperialist bourgeoisie. The Cadets called themselves the party of "people's freedom" but in fact tried to make a deal with the autocracy in order to retain tsarism as a constitutional monarchy. Throughout the imperialist war (1914-18) they demanded "war to victory". After the February Revolution, by conspiring with the S.R. and Menshevik leaders of the Petrograd Soviet, they acquired a leading position in the Provisional Government and conducted an anti-popular counter-revolutionary policy. After the Great October Socialist Revolution they played the role of agents and mercenaries of foreign imperialism and were the organisers of internal forces of counter-revolution. Lenin called the Cadet Party the all-Russia headquarters of the counter-revolution. p. 66

[39] *Rech* (Speech)—the central organ of the Cadet Party, published daily in St. Petersburg from February 1906. Closed down by the Revolutionary Military Committee of the Petrograd Soviet on October 26 (November 8), 1917; it was published under other names until August 1918.   p. 66

[40] *Pravda* (The Truth)—the legal daily newspaper of the Bolshevik Party published in St. Petersburg. It was founded on the initiative of the St. Petersburg workers in April 1912. *Pravda* was a workers' paper for the masses and was published with funds collected by the workers themselves. A wide circle of worker correspondents and worker writers formed around the paper. In one year of publication over 11,000 items by worker correspondents appeared in its columns. Its average circulation was 40,000 but in some months the number sold went as high as 60,000 a day. When Lenin was abroad he exercised guidance over the paper, wrote to it almost daily, gave instructions to its editorial board and recruited the best writers in the Party to work for it. *Pravda* was incessantly persecuted by the police. During the first year of its existence it was confiscated

41 times and 36 court cases were instituted against its editors who spent a total of $47^1/_2$ months in prison. In the course of two years and three months *Pravda* was closed down by the government eight times but it again appeared under other names: *Rabochaya Pravda, Severnaya Pravda, Pravda Truda, Za Pravdu, Proletarskaya Pravda, Put Pravdy, Rabochy, Trudovaya Pravda.* On July 8 (21), 1914, on the eve of the First World War, the paper was closed down and its publication was not resumed until after the February Revolution.

Since March 5 (18), 1917, *Pravda* has been published as the central organ of the R.S.D.L.P. On April 5 (18), on his return from abroad, Lenin joined the editorial board of *Pravda* and took over its leadership. On July 5 (18), 1917 the *Pravda* editorial offices were raided by officer cadets and Cossacks. Between July and October 1917, *Pravda* was persecuted by the Provisional Government and constantly changed its name, appearing as *Listok "Pravdy", Proletary, Rabochy, Rabochy Put.* Since October 27 (November 9), 1917, the newspaper has been published under its old name of *Pravda.* p. 66

41 *Shlyakhi* (Paths)—organ of the Ukrainian Students' Union, nationalist in trend; published in Lvov from April 1913 to March 1914.
p. 66

42 *Novoye Vremya* (New Times)—a daily newspaper published in St. Petersburg from 1868 to October 1917. Began as a moderate liberal paper but after 1876 turned into an organ of the reactionary nobility and civil-service bureaucrats. The paper conducted a struggle against the bourgeois-liberal movement as well as against the revolutionary movement; from 1905 it was one of the organs of the Black Hundreds. Lenin called *Novoye Vremya* an example of a venal newspaper.

Zemshchina (Land Affairs)—a Black-Hundred daily newspaper, organ of the extreme Right-wing deputies to the State Duma; published in St. Petersburg from July 1909 to February 1917. p. 68

43 *"Grab 'em and hold 'em"*—an expression of police arbitrariness taken from Gleb Uspensky's "Sentry Box". p. 69

44 *Kievskaya Mysl* (Kiev Thought)—a liberal-bourgeois daily, published from December 1906 to December 1918 in Kiev. The Menshevik liquidators were close collaborators with the paper. p. 70

45 *Constable Mymretsov*—a character from Gleb Uspensky's "Sentry Box", a vulgar and ignorant policeman in a small provincial town in tsarist Russia. p. 71

46 This expression is taken from A. S. Griboyedov's comedy *Wit Works Woe.* p. 73

47 *Naprzód* (Forward)—the central organ of the Polish Social-Democratic Party in Galicia and Silesia, published in Cracow from 1892.
p. 75

[48] Lenin refers here to W. Liebknecht's reminiscences of Marx (see the symposium *Reminiscences of Marx and Engels*, Moscow, 1957, p. 98). p. 85

[49] See Marx's letter to Engels, July 5, 1870. p. 85

[50] See Marx and Engels, *Selected Correspondence*, Moscow, 1965, pp. 149, 177-78, 178-79. p. 87

[51] See Marx's letter to Engels, December 17, 1867. p. 88

[52] See Marx and Engels, *On Britain*, Moscow, 1953, p. 501. p. 89

[53] Quoted from Plekhanov's article "The Draft Programme of the Russian Social-Democratic Party" published in *Zarya* No. 4 for 1902. p. 92

[54] *Borba* (Struggle)—Trotsky's magazine published in St. Petersburg from February to July 1914. Masquerading as a "non-factionalist" Trotsky conducted a campaign against Lenin and the Bolshevik Party in the columns of the magazine. p. 97

[55] Lenin quotes an expression from *Sketches of Seminary Life*, by the Russian writer N. G. Pomyalovsky. p. 98

[56] These words are from a Sevastopol soldiers' song about an action on the Chornaya River on August 4, 1855, during the Crimean War. The author of the song was Lev Tolstoi. p. 100

[57] *Russkoye Bogatstvo* (Russian Wealth)—a monthly magazine published in St. Petersburg from 1876 to the middle of 1918. From the beginning of the nineties the magazine was the organ of the liberal Narodniks. From 1906 the magazine actually became an organ of the semi-Cadet People's Socialist Party. Lenin defined the trend followed by *Russkoye Bogatstvo* at this time as "Narodnik, Narodnik-Cadet". p. 102

[58] *Council of the United Nobility*—counter-revolutionary association of landed proprietors formed in May 1906. It exerted considerable influence on government policy. At the time of the Third Duma a large number of its members belonged to the State Council and guiding centres of the Black-Hundred organisations. p. 106

[59] The quotation is from Chernyshevsky's novel *Prologue*. p. 106

[60] See F. Engels, *Emigré Literature. I. The Polish Proclamation.* (*Der Volksstaat* No. 73, 1874.) p. 107

[61] *Dreyfus case*—a provocative trial instituted in 1894 by reactionary royalist circles among the French militarists against the Jewish General Staff officer Dreyfus who was falsely accused of espionage and high treason. A court martial condemned Dreyfus to life impris-

onment. The public movement for a re-examination of the Dreyfus case that developed in France took the form of a fierce struggle between the republicans and the royalists and led to the eventual release of Dreyfus in 1906.

Lenin called the Dreyfus case "one of the many thousands of fraudulent tricks of the reactionary military clique". p. 113

[62] The incident took place in the town of Zabern (Alsace) in November 1913. It was caused by the brutality of a Prussian officer towards the Alsatians. It gave rise to an outburst of indignation among the local, mainly French, population, directed against the Prussian militarists. (See Lenin's article "Zabern" in *Collected Works*, Vol. 19, pp. 513-15.) p. 113

[63] See Marx's letter to Engels, November 30, 1867 (Marx and Engels, *Selected Correspondence*, Moscow, 1965, pp. 194-95 and 195-97).
p. 113

[64] Lenin criticised the reactionary idea of "cultural-national autonomy", advanced by Renner and Bauer, in an article entitled "Cultural-National Autonomy" (*Collected Works*, Vol. 19, pp. 503-07) and in his "Critical Remarks on the National Question" (*Collected Works*, Vol. 20, pp. 17-51 and present booklet, pp. 12-44). p. 114

[65] See Marx's letter to Engels, November 2, 1867 (no English translation available). p. 117

[66] *Die Glocke* (The Bell)—a magazine published first in Munich and then in Berlin from 1915 to 1925 by Parvus (Helfand), member of the German Social-Democratic Party, a social-chauvinist and agent of German imperialism. p. 117

[67] Friedrich Engels, "Der demokratische Panslawismus". Lenin used *Aus dem literarischen Nachlass von Karl Marx, Friedrich Engels und Ferdinand Lassalle*, hrsg. von Franz Mehring, Stuttgart, 1902, Bd. III, S. 246-64, in which the author of the article is not named.
p. 117

[68] Lenin refers here to the resolution on the national question which he wrote and which was adopted at the conference of the Central Committee of the R.S.D.L.P. and leading Party workers held between October 6 and 14 (N.S.), 1913 at Poronin, near Cracow. For reasons of secrecy the conference was called the "Summer" or "August" Conference. The resolution is published in Lenin's *Collected Works*, Vol. 19, pp. 427-29. p. 122

[69] *Nashe Dyelo* (Our Cause)—a monthly Menshevik magazine, chief organ of the liquidators and social-chauvinists in Russia; published in 1915 in Petrograd in place of the magazine *Nasha Zarya* (Our Dawn) that had been closed down in October 1914. p. 122

[70] *Zimmerwald Conference*—the first international socialist conference at Zimmerwald, held September 5-8, 1915, where a struggle developed between the revolutionary internationalists headed by Lenin and the Kautskyite majority. Lenin formed the Zimmerwald Left from the Left internationalists; the Bolshevik Party adopted the only correct and consistently internationalist position against the war.

The conference issued a manifesto declaring the world war to be an imperialist war, condemned the behaviour of the "socialists" who voted for war credits and took part in bourgeois governments and appealed to the workers of Europe to develop the struggle against war and strive for a peace without annexations and indemnities.

The conference also passed a resolution expressing sympathy with the victims of the war, and elected an International Socialist Commission. p. 122

[71] *Vorbote* (Herald)—the theoretical magazine of the Zimmerwald Left published in Berne (in German) in 1916. Two issues appeared, No. 1 in January and No. 2 in April 1916. The magazine printed Lenin's "Opportunism and the Collapse of the Second International" and "The Socialist Revolution and the Right of Nations to Self-Determination (Theses)" (see V. I. Lenin, *Collected Works*, Vol. 22, pp. 108-20, 143-56 and present pamphlet, pp. 110-24). p. 125

[72] *Theses on Imperialism and National Oppression* were compiled by the editors of *Gazeta Robotnicza* and published in the *Sbornik Sotsial-Demokrata* (Social-Democrat's Symposium) No. 1 in October 1916. p. 125

[73] For an assessment of these three viewpoints on Polish independence see Lenin's "The Right of Nations to Self-Determination", in this booklet, pp. 45-104. p. 125

[74] Lenin refers here to the discussion that took place in 1903 in connection with the elaboration of the R.S.D.L.P. programme that was adopted at the Second Congress of the Party (see V. I. Lenin, *Collected Works*, Vol. 6, "Material for the Preparation of the Programme of the R.S.D.L.P.", "The National Question in Our Programme", pp. 17-78, 454-63) and the 1913 discussion between the Bolsheviks on the one side and the liquidators. Trotskyites and Bund members on the other on the question of "cultural-national autonomy" (see V. I. Lenin, *Collected Works*, Vol. 19, "The National Programme of the R.S.D.L.P.", pp. 539-45 and Vol. 20, "Critical Remarks on the National Question", pp. 17-51). p. 126

[75] See Marx and Engels, *Selected Works*, Moscow, 1962, Vol. II, pp. 32-33. p. 128

[76] See F. Engels's article "Po and Rhein". p. 128

[77] The German "Internationale" Group, later renamed the Spartacus League, was formed at the beginning of the First World War by German Left Social-Democrats—Karl Liebknecht, Rosa Luxemburg, Franz Mehring, Klara Zetkin and others. The "Internationale" Group played an important and positive role in the history of the German working-class movement. In January 1916, at an all-German Conference of Left Social-Democrats, the group adopted the theses prepared by Rosa Luxemburg on the tasks of international Social-Democracy. The "Internationale" Group conducted propaganda among the masses against the imperialist war and exposed the predatory policy of German imperialism and the treachery of the Social-Democratic leaders. But the group did not rid itself of its serious errors in important questions of theory and policy: it rejected the principle of the self-determination of nations in its Marxist interpretation (i.e., up to and including separation and the formation of independent states), denied the possibility of national wars of liberation in the epoch of imperialism, underestimated the role of the revolutionary party, etc. A criticism of the mistakes of the German Left is given in Lenin's "The Junius Pamphlet" (see Collected Works, Vol. 22, pp. 305-19). "The Military Programme of the Proletarian Revolution" (see Collected Works, Vol. 23, pp. 77-87) and other writings. In 1917 the "Internationale" Group joined the Centrist Independent Social-Democratic Party of Germany, retaining its organisational independence. After the revolution in Germany in November 1918 the group broke away from the "independents" and in December of that year formed the Communist Party of Germany. p. 136

[78] Junius—Rosa Luxemburg. p. 136

[79] See Friedrich Engels, "Der demokratische Panslawismus", in Neue Rheinische Zeitung Nos. 222 and 223, February 15 and 16, 1849 (no English translation available). p. 144

[80] See Engels's article: "What Have the Working Classes to Do with Poland?", Section II, in Commonwealth of March 24 and 31, and May 5, 1866. p. 147

[81] Lichtstrahlen (Rays of Light)—monthly magazine, organ of a group of Left Social-Democrats in Germany edited by J. Borchardt. Appeared irregulary between 1913 and 1921 in Berlin. p. 154

[82] Berner Tagwacht (Berne Sentinel)—a daily newspaper, organ of the Swiss Social-Democratic Party, founded in Berne in 1893. p. 154

[83] The article referred to is Rosa Luxemburg's "The National Question and Autonomy", published in Nos. 6, 7, 8, 9, 10, 12 and 14-15 of Przeglad Socjaldemokratyczny (Social-Democratic Review) for 1908 and 1909. p. 154

[84] See Note 22. p. 155

[85] See Marx and Engels, *Selected Correspondence*, Moscow, 1965, p. 351.   p. 157

[86] *Nashe Slovo* (Our Word)—a Menshevik-Trotskyite daily newspaper published in Paris from January 1915 to September 1916, replacing the newspaper *Golos* (The Voice).   p. 158

[87] *K. R.*—Karl Radek.   p. 159

[88] The reference to the followers of the Menshevik K. A. Gvozdyov, a representative of the "workers' group" on the Central War Industries Committee who opposed the strike movement of the workers and openly supported the imperialist bourgeoisie.   p. 164

[89] The letter published under the title of "The Question of Nationalities or 'Autonomisation'" is a continuation of the notes dictated by Lenin in December 1922—"Letter to the Congress" (known as "The Testament") and "Granting Legislative Functions to the State Planning Commission".

Lenin attached extraordinary significance to the correct conduct of national policy and to the practical implementation of the Declaration and the Treaties adopted by the Congress of Soviets, and on December 30 and 31, 1922, dictated this letter. It was read at a meeting of the leaders of delegations to the Twelfth Congress of the R.C.P.(B.) that took place in April 1923. The Congress adopted a resolution on the national question based on Lenin's letter.

Autonomisation—the idea to unite the Soviet Republics through their entry into the R.S.F.S.R. on the principle of autonomy. This was at the basis of the "Draft Resolution on Mutual Relations of the R.S.F.S.R. and Independent Republics", which was proposed by Stalin and adopted, in September 1922, by a C.C. commission set up to work out for the C.C. plenum the question of further relationships between the R.S.F.S.R., the Ukrainian Republic, the Byelorussian Republic and the Transcaucasian Federation. In a letter to the members of the Political Bureau on September 26, 1922, Lenin seriously criticised the project. He proposed a totally different solution of the question, namely, voluntary union of all the Soviet Republics, including the R.S.F.S.R., in a new state entity, the Union of Soviet Republics, based on complete equality.

He wrote: "We recognise ourselves equal with the Ukrainian Republic, and the others, and join the new union, the new federation together with them and on an equal footing...." The C.C. Commission, in accordance with Lenin's instructions, revised the draft resolution, which was approved by a Plenary Meeting of the Central Committee in October 1922. Preparatory work for the unification of the Republics was started on the basis of the C.C. decision. On December 30, 1922, the First Congress of Soviets of the U.S.S.R. adopted its historic decision on the formation of the Union of Soviet Socialist Republics.   p. 165

[90] The Plenary Meetings of the Central Committee of the R.C.P.(B.), held in October and December of 1922. The agendas of the meetings contained questions on the formation of the U.S.S.R.   p. 165